Ghosts of Hollywood

The Show Still Goes On

Marla Brooks

with Foreword
by *Most Haunted*'s David Wells

4880 Lower Valley Road, Atglen, Pennsylvania 19310

Schiffer Books are available at special discounts for bulk purchases for sales promotions or premiums. Special editions, including personalized covers, corporate imprints, and excerpts can be created in large quantities for special needs. For more information contact the publisher:

Published by Schiffer Publishing Ltd.
4880 Lower Valley Road
Atglen, PA 19310
Phone: (610) 593-1777; Fax: (610) 593-2002
E-mail: Info@schifferbooks.com

For the largest selection of fine reference books on this and related subjects, please visit our web site at **www.schifferbooks.com**. We are always looking for people to write books on new and related subjects. If you have an idea for a book please contact us at the above address.

This book may be purchased from the publisher.
Include $3.95 for shipping.
Please try your bookstore first.
You may write for a free catalog.

In Europe, Schiffer books are distributed by
Bushwood Books
6 Marksbury Ave.
Kew Gardens
Surrey TW9 4JF England
Phone: 44 (0) 20 8392-8585; Fax: 44 (0) 20 8392-9876
E-mail: info@bushwoodbooks.co.uk
Website: www.bushwoodbooks.co.uk
Free postage in the U.K., Europe; air mail at cost.

Copyright © 2008 by Marla Brooks
Library of Congress Control Number: 2007938207

Designed by Mark David Bowyer
Type set in A Charming Font Expanded / NewBskvll BT

ISBN: 978-0-7643-2883-1
Printed in China

Dedication

To my parents and grandparents who keep a watchful and loving eye on me from the other side, and to my spirit guides who always manage to point me in the right direction and keep me safe.

Acknowledgments

If it weren't for the help of some very talented individuals, this book would still just be a wild idea floating around in my head with nowhere to go. Thanks to David Wells, Chris Fleming, and Kenny Kingston for their wisdom and willingness to share some of it with me, to Victoria Gross and Barry Conrad, both wonderfully talented paranormal investigators who cheerfully came along for the ride and worked their butts off in the process, and to Hollywood historian Scott Michaels who let me pick his brain whenever necessary. Much appreciation also goes to everyone who not only invited us into their haunted world to investigate their resident ghosts and patiently sat for interviews about their experiences, and to Donna Harris at the Catalina Chamber of Commerce for going that extra mile.

I'd also like to thank Dinah Roseberry at Schiffer Books who not only gave me the opportunity to write this book in the first place, but also offered tons of encouragement and invaluable assistance every step of the way.

Author Note

W hile most people may not openly admit it, virtually all of us believe in ghosts. There is probably not a person alive who hasn't either experienced some sort of paranormal encounter or spoken to someone who has. That is why books, movies, and television programs devoted to this phenomenon have always delivered enthusiastic audiences.

Much has been written about Hollywood ghosts, but what sets this book apart is that many of the true accounts of Hollywood hauntings have never been written about before and are told by the people who experience them on a daily basis. The book often takes readers off the much-beaten path to include new locations, first-hand investigations, and new information on Hollywood haunts from several of your favorite and most well-respected psychics, including *Most Haunted's* David Wells, Chris Fleming of *Dead Famous* fame, and Psychic to the Stars, Kenny Kingston.

This comprehensive book not only contains information about Hollywood ghosts and hauntings, but also offers historical background about both the locations and the restless spirits who inhabit them. It will be of great interest to history buffs, Hollywood buffs, and avid ghost hunters alike.

Foreword

I t seems that lately our world with all it's joys and beauty just isn't enough for some, and the complex world of ghostly activity calls to us from beyond the veil; odd when you think we'll all have our chance to see it soon enough!

Still we pursue the truth of who we are, who we *truly* are, not this physical self, this bag of bones and chemicals built by magic and fast food, surely if we see evidence of the survival of others, that must mean we too survive—flawless logic.

This new national sport of ghost investigations become even more interesting when you add the long established art of celebrity watching, a combination that proves irresistible to many.

Access to those, who in life most of us would have no opportunity of meeting, seems incredible and, to be honest, it must beg the question: Why would Lucille Ball want to talk to Aunt Fred and Uncle Harry on a visit to her old sound stage?

Maybe Lucille is bored in heaven, what an awful thought, or perhaps she isn't anyone special in the astral worlds and needs her fix of adulation to help her sleep at night? Who knows why the famous and the infamous return and beg to be seen; maybe that's a question you should ask when next you meet such a person? Trauma, intense emotions such as love or hate and even vengeance can tie a spirit to its surroundings, and Hollywood has its share of all of them.

Respect is the key to success when talking to even the most awkward astral character. They may be grumpy, they may have a point to make and only want to make it by throwing things rather than through civilized conversation, but they know something you don't know for sure: that the soul survives and evidence of that is in their hands.

Never having met a celebrity ghost yet, I live in hope. The closest I have come are historical figures such as Oliver Cromwell who was rather annoying and full of his own importance, but still I managed to get some small details from him that confirmed his identity, and when pushed, he responded by pushing harder—a reminder that knowing what you are dealing with and how to deal with it is important. You may think your favourite actor or actress will welcome you with open arms, and they may, but don't take any chances—know your craft.

This book explores more recent history which makes it easier to identify not only the characters involved, but also to verify the information they give. Going back hundreds of years can mean the Chinese whisper syndrome has changed many things; going back less than a hundred means accuracy is better, although not guaranteed. Maybe those Hollywood *PR* folks still accompany their stars in the afterlife—who knows!

Whilst walking around Hollywood you can't help but think of all those famous feet that have walked there before you, of the souls that have now passed but might just return to their favourite haunts—sorry, it had to be said.

Whilst investigating the Hollywood American Legion Hall, I sat where Clark Gable would have sat, leaned against the bar Marilyn Monroe would have ordered her drink over, and even though they weren't there, I could feel them in the air, smell Marilyn's perfume and pausing for second, I could have sworn I heard a whisper in the air.

We can't pick and choose who we talk with, but we can put ourselves into the places these departed souls are likely to come back to, if indeed they wanted to, and here you may pick up on the residual energy of how it was in their day and live among their energy even for a short while. And if you're lucky, the respect you show for them maybe rewarded with more, even if it is only fleeting…

—David Wells

Contents

Introduction

Back in 1853, long before the advent of the motion picture industry, all that stood on the site that was to become Hollywood was a single adobe hut.

Hollywood was once part of two large Spanish land-grant ranchos, Rancho LaBrea to the west and Rancho Los Feliz to the east. The first permanent settlers in the area were cattle ranchers until a severe drought in 1860 forced many to sell their holdings. By 1870, many of the larger tracts had been subdivided and an agricultural community began to flourish, raising mainly hay and grains. The land around Santa Monica Boulevard was considered the most fertile, while the land north of Sunset was reserved for sheep grazing. Later it was found that this grazing land lay in a climate zone ideal for subtropical fruits and winter vegetables, so farmers began cultivating bananas, pineapples, and others of that ilk.

In 1886, H. H. Wilcox, an ambitious real estate investor from Kansas bought 160 acres of land in the countryside and christened it "Hollywood" with a little help from his wife, Daeda. Hollywood was the name of the summer home of a woman Mrs. Wilcox had sat beside on a train, and she liked the sound of it.

Wilcox soon drew up a grid map for the town which he filed with the county recorder's office on February 1, 1887. That date marked the first official appearance of the name Hollywood on any legal document. Wilcox carved out Prospect Avenue for the main street, lined it and the other wide dirt avenues with pepper trees, and began selling large residential lots to wealthy Midwesterners looking to build homes so they could "winter in California." Within a few years, Prospect Avenue became a prestigious residential street populated with large Queen Anne, Victorian, and Mission Revival houses.

By the turn of the twentieth century, Hollywood boasted 500 residents and had its own post office, newspaper, hotel, and two markets. The city was incorporated as a municipality in 1903, and among the town ordinances was one prohibiting the sale of liquor, except by pharmacists, and another outlawing the driving of cattle through the streets in herds of more than two hundred.

A new trolley car track running from the city of Los Angeles, which was seven miles east through the citrus groves, was installed in 1904, and the system was called "the Hollywood boulevard." Then in 1910, because of an ongoing struggle to secure an adequate water supply, the townsmen voted for Hollywood to be annexed into the City of Los Angeles, and with annexation, the name of Prospect Avenue was formally changed to Hollywood Boulevard.

At about the same time, motion picture production companies from New York and New Jersey began moving to California because of the reliable weather and the wide variety of natural scenery which would come in handy during film-making.

The Biograph Company sent director D. W. Griffith and a troop of actors including Lillian Gish, Mary Pickford, and Lionel Barrymore to the west coast in 1910. They began filming on a vacant lot near Georgia Street in Downtown Los

Angeles and then decided to explore new territories. They traveled several miles north to a little village that was friendly and whose residents seemed to enjoy the novelty of a movie company filming there. This is where Griffith shot the first movie ever made in Hollywood, *In Old California*. The rest, as they say, is movie-making history, and where there is history, there are sure to be ghosts.

In his sixteenth century pastoral comedy, *As You Like It*, William Shakespeare wrote, "All the world's a stage, and all the men and women merely players." But here in twenty-first century Hollywood, many of our most famous dearly departed players still aren't ready to take their final bows. While some of these celebrated specters are no doubt happy to be remembered for their body of work, it's their out-of-body appearances that garner the most interest these days.

Tourists from all over the world flock to Hollywood to see where the movie stars live, but lots of folks are also curious about where they died, and more importantly, where their spirits remain. But why are they still here?

The most obvious answer to that question is, "Because they want to be," but spirits remain earthbound or come back in visitation for a number of reasons. Sometimes the emotional shock brought on by a sudden passing or great emotional suffering at the time of death is all it takes to keep someone from making the final transition from this world to the next. A good example of this type of haunting takes place at the Virginia Hill house in Beverly Hills. Psychics have reported seeing the spirit of notorious gangster Bugsy Siegel cowering in fear amid a hail of phantom bullets, reliving his final moments on earth over and over again.

Not all Hollywood hauntings are the result of a violent act, however. Some celebrity ghosts, like Groucho Marx, just seem to love their work. Groucho is said to make nightly appearances at his old office above The Laugh Factory comedy club on the Sunset Strip. Over at Paramount Studios, it is believed that comedian Redd Foxx, who died of a massive heart attack on Stage 31 while rehearsing for his television show, *The Royal Family,* in October of 1991, continues to report to work each day as usual. Paramount also happens to share a wall with the Hollywood Forever Cemetery where many of the studio's former employees are buried. Some of these long-dead workers are regularly seen walking directly through the wall from one lot to the next.

Hollywood also boasts a number of very haunted houses. The ghosts of Joan Crawford, Ozzie Nelson, TV's Superman George Reeves, Rudolph Valentino, and Lucille Ball all seem to subscribe to the adage, "There's no place like home," and reportedly make regular visits to their beloved abodes to keep an eye on the new tenants. But it's not just celebrity houses that are haunted.

I've had the dubious pleasure of living in haunted houses all my life, and my current home, as well as several others in this old Hollywood neighborhood seem to have their fair share of ghosts. From things that go bump in the night to being touched by unseen hands to full-blown apparitions, we've pretty much seen it all. So what is it about this city that keeps these lively spirits around? Are there old ties that bind? Scores to settle? A yearning for the "good old days?" Whatever the reason, the ghosts of Hollywood are alive and well, relatively speaking, and most of us who live here wouldn't have it any other way.

A handful of the locations I have written about are well-known for their resident ghosts while others have seldom, if ever, been written about. In some cases, like with Boardner's Bar, The Hollywood Center Studios, and The Ricardo Montalban Theater, I've also enlisted the help of some well-known psychics who have either previously explored these haunted locations on their own or have come along with me to verify reported ghostly activity. While the majority of our ghostly encounters on these outings were not with famous spirits, they were fascinating nonetheless. We ran the gamut from those benevolent entities who were sticking around to protect the people and places they haunt to a couple of dark, malevolent energies who were up to no good.

Most of the hauntings take place in Hollywood proper, but in case I go off the beaten path here and there, it's because, after all, Hollywood is not just a place. It's also a state of mind and extends to anywhere celebrities live, breathe, and ultimately, die.

One final note: A great many of the locations I've written about in this book are public venues and they welcome visitors, but some are private homes whose residents will probably not appreciate any more "uninvited" guests. So please do not trespass on private property or in any other way disturb the occupants of these homes, whether they be living...or dead.

The Ghosts of Laurel Canyon, the Hollywood Hills and the Hills of Beverly

Laurel Canyon is a self-contained canyon neighborhood with many side roads that branch off the main canyon. The area was first settled in the 1920s and became a part of Los Angeles in 1923. Prior to major development, Laurel Canyon was a secluded valley that supplied water to farms at the base of the canyon and to some hillside grazing for local sheep ranchers.

With the creation of the Hollywood film industry in 1910, the canyon attracted a host of celebrities of the day including Wally Reid, Tom Mix, Clara Bow, Ramon Novarro, Harry Houdini, and Bessie Love. Errol Flynn once lived in a huge mansion just north of Houdini's estate and many of these English Tudor and Spanish style homes are still lived in today.

By the 1920s, the area had been transformed into a proper community with its own one-room schoolhouse, a local newspaper, a grocery store, and several restaurants. Unlike other canyon neighborhoods, Laurel Canyon has houses lining one side of the main street most of the way up to Mulholland Drive. Some of the main side streets include Mount Olympus, Kirkwood, Wonderland, and Lookout Mountain Avenue.

The Canyon was the focal point of the Psychedelic Rock movement of the 60s and 70s, and during that era, it was second only to Haight-Ashbury as a Mecca for hippies. Frank Zappa's rented cabin at Lookout Mountain and Laurel Canyon Boulevard, now a vacant lot, was the center of Laurel Canyon's crazed rock scene. Musicians who made appearances at the lower cabin that was once home to silent film star Tom Mix and at the upper Tree House that was designed by famed architect Robert Byrd in the 1920s included Jimi Hendrix, The Doors, Janis Joplin, James Taylor, and Mick Jagger.

The bohemian spirit from that time still lingers today, and every year residents gather for a group photograph at the canyon's country market, The Canyon Store. Jim Morrison's old house, which was recently remodeled, is just behind the Country Store and next door to the Canyon Cleaners.

For the most part, Laurel Canyon is a lovely, friendly, (and somewhat pricey) place to live, but over the years, some very unsavory events have taken place that have not only left a mark on the otherwise peaceful nature of the area, but a few unhappy ghosts as well.

The Wonderland Murders — 8763 Wonderland Drive

The Wonderland Murders have been described as one of the bloodiest mass murders in California history and it's been said that the tormented spirits of the murder victims still remain, perhaps trying to avenge their horrible deaths.

The 2003 film *Wonderland* chronicled the grisly murders, also known as "Four on the Floor" or "Laurel Canyon Murders" that took place in the early morning hours of July 1, 1981. The crime was allegedly masterminded by reputed gangster Eddie Nash, a Los Angeles nightclub and restaurant owner. Also involved was the "larger-than-life" porn star John C. Holmes.

The Wonderland Gang was comprised of three people, Joy Audrey Gold Miller, William R. DeVerell (Miller and DeVerell were a couple), and their leader Ronald Launius, who were all reputed drug users and dealers. They lived in a rented house at 8763 Wonderland Avenue.

On June 28, 1981, the trio got together with two other unsavory types, David Lind and Tracy McCourt, and John Holmes, who used to buy drugs from them. During their visit, the group decided to rob the home of wealthy Eddie Nash (aka Adel Nasrallah) who reportedly was also in the drug trade. Shortly thereafter, Holmes paid a visit to his friend Nash under the guise of buying drugs. While he was there, Holmes scouted out the house and managed to unlock a back door without Nash's knowledge. The next morning, DeVerell, Lanius, Lind, and McCourt went to Nash's house. While McCourt stayed in the car, a stolen Ford Granada, the other three entered through the previously unlocked door. They took Nash and his live-in bodyguard, Gregory DeWitt Diles, by surprise and handcuffed them. Then, after looting the house of money, drugs, and jewelry, the group fled the scene and returned to Wonderland Avenue to split up the loot, shortchanging Holmes and McCourt in the process.

Nash suspected that Holmes had been involved in the robbery and after he managed to free himself and his bodyguard, he ordered Diles to go get Holmes and bring him to back to the house. The porn star was found on the street in Hollywood, wearing one of Nash's stolen rings.

Nash had Diles beat up Holmes until he identified the people behind the crime. This beating was witnessed by Scott Thorson, then-boyfriend of Liberace, who, at the time, happened to be picking up drugs at Nash's house.

In the early morning hours of July 1, 1981, two days after the robbery and the day after Holmes' confession, Miller, De-Verell, Launius, Launius' wife Susan, and Barbara Richardson (Lind's girlfriend) were bludgeoned repeatedly with striated steel pipes. Susan Launius survived with serious injuries, but the other four were killed. Veteran LAPD detectives who arrived at the house after the murders claimed they had never seen so much blood at one crime scene.

John Holmes was present at the murder site, as evidenced by his finger prints, but it is unknown whether he actually participated in any of the killings.

According to court testimony, David Lind managed to survive the attack because he had spent the night at a San Fernando Valley motel, consuming drugs with a prostitute. Shortly after the news media reported the murders, Lind contacted the police and pointed the finger at Nash and Holmes. LAPD detectives Tom Lange and Robert Souza, who were to work on the O. J. Simpson murder case thirteen years later, lead the murder investigation.

When police searched Nash's home, they found more than a million dollars in cocaine, and Nash ended up spending two years in prison. Holmes was charged with the murders, but his lawyer, Earl Hanson, successfully presented Holmes as one of the victims, and Holmes was acquitted on June 16,

1982. He refused to testify and cooperate with authorities and spent some time in jail for contempt of court.

Holmes died of AIDS in 1988, at a Veteran's Administration Medical Center in Los Angeles. After his death, his first wife, Sharon Gebenini-Holmes, came forward and said that he had come to her house in the early morning after the killings with blood splattered all over his clothes, but did not explain why.

In 1990, Nash was charged in state court with having planned the murders and Diles was charged for his participation in them. Scott Thorson testified against them, but the trial ended with an 11-1 hung jury. A second trial in 1991 ended in acquittal. Diles died in 1995.

In 2000, after a four-year joint investigation involving both local and federal authorities, Eddie Nash was arrested and indicted on federal charges under the RICO act for running a drug dealing and money laundering operation, conspiring to carry out the Wonderland Murders, and bribing one of the jurors in his first trial. Nash, already in his seventies and suffering from emphysema and several other ailments, agreed to a plea bargain agreement in September 2001. He admitted to bribing the lone holdout in his first trial with $50,000. He also pleaded guilty to the RICO charges and to money laundering. He admitted to having ordered his associates to retrieve stolen property from the Wonderland house, which might have resulted in violence including murder, yet he denied having planned the murders that took place. He received a four and a half year prison sentence and a $250,000 fine.

As for the murder victims themselves, one can only hope that they've now found peace, but since hauntings are common when people die under tragic circumstances, it's very likely that the property on Wonderland Avenue may still be quite active.

Ramon Novarro's Death House — 3110 Laurel Canyon Boulevard

Another gruesome murder that took place in Laurel Canyon involved silent screen heartthrob Ramon Novarro.

The son of a prosperous Mexican dentist who went on to achieve fame as a Latin Lover in silent films, Ramon Novarro, born José Ramón Gil Samaniego in Durango, Mexico, on February 6, 1899, moved to California with his family to escape the 1910 revolution in his country. Because the family's wealth had been left behind, young Novarro took on a number of odd jobs, ranging from piano teacher to cabaret singer. He toured vaudeville in a musical act, and in 1917 began picking up extra and bit work in Hollywood. When he was eventually cast as the lovable scoundrel Rupert of Hentzau in director Rex Ingram's *The Prisoner of Zenda* in 1922, Novarro scored an immediate hit and was promptly built up by the Hollywood press agent brigade as "the New Valentino."

Novarro achieved his greatest success in 1925 as the star of *Ben-Hur*, a role which elevated him into the Hollywood elite, and with Rudolph Valentino's untimely death in 1926, he became the screen's leading Latin actor. He was popular as a swashbuckler in action roles, and was also considered one of the great romantic lead actors of his day.

The downside to Novarro's seemingly charmed existence was that he had struggled all his life as a result of his conflicting views over his Roman Catholic religion and his homosexuality although Rudolph Valentino's close friend, Jimmy Quirk, wrote that Novarro was far more relaxed and accepting of his sexuality than was Valentino.

There are rumors that MGM mogul Louis B. Mayer tried to coerce Novarro into a "lavender marriage," (like Rock Hudson would consent to many years later for the sake of his career) but he refused. Some claim there is no evidence that Mayer tried to coerce Novarro into contractual marriage, but Novarro himself intimated as much in interviews late in his life.

There were many in 1920s Hollywood who knew Novarro was homosexual, but he was widely considered a gentleman, a class act that kept his private life private. He once said in an interview that in the 1920s, many stars were allowed their privacy — that the details of their personal lives were not published unless they sought it.

At he peak of his success in the late 1920s and early 1930s, the actor was earning more than $100,000 per film, but after starring in a number of musicals for MGM and being badly miscast in a series of films, Novarro decided to leave show business, and because he had wisely invested his earnings over the years, the actor was able to maintain a comfortable lifestyle without having to work.

Novarro met his maker on Halloween 1968 when his heightened libido clouded his judgment. On that date the sixty-nice-year-old Novarro invited two street hustlers, brothers Paul and Tom Ferguson, into his Laurel Canyon home for a bit of fun. Apparently he'd been seeing twenty-two-year-old Paul for several weeks, and seventeen-year-old Tom had recently come to town. Over the course of the next few hours, Novarro was murdered by the brothers and died a tortuous death as the result of asphyxiation. He choked to death on his own blood after a brutal beating and his battered body was found the next morning by a servant.

The brothers were soon apprehended, and during their trial it was revealed that the two young men believed that a large sum of money was hidden in Novarro's house and that's what they were after. The prosecution accused them of torturing the actor for several hours to force him to reveal where the nonexistent money was hidden. They left with a mere twenty dollars that they took from his bathrobe pocket before fleeing the scene.

Both brothers were convicted of murder and sentenced to life in prison, but were paroled after serving only seven years.

In 1980, a young actor who owned the secluded canyon home turned it into a shrine for the dead star, and many people who visited the house told of an eerie feeling surrounding it. A new home was built on the site in 1991, but some say that Novarro still haunts the ill-fated property.

The Houdini Mansion — 2398 Laurel Canyon Boulevard

By the time famed magician Harry Houdini had moved to Laurel Canyon, he was already a rich and famous celebrity, but he came to California to further his fortune in the Hollywood film industry. According to lore, the mansion he purchased was cursed even before Houdini bought the property in the 1920s. A murder in 1918 started the chain of events, and all those who lived in the house from then on were plagued by bad luck and disasters. Although Houdini spent very little time at his lavish estate on Laurel Canyon Boulevard before his untimely death on Halloween night in 1926, some say the curse got him, too.

The magician had been in the middle of a U. S. tour in the fall of 1926 with his wife, Bess, when he and she both began to experience severe stomach discomfort. The consummate performer refused medical treatment because that would have meant missing some shows. Houdini was possibly suffering from the onset of appendicitis and his own stubborn refusal to see a doctor might have been the beginning of the end.

Houdini was tired and unusually accident-prone during the tour, and while in Albany, New York, he broke his ankle during one of his shows as he was being lifted into the Water Torture Cell. Despite the pain, he continued his performances. In Canada a few days later, he was allegedly punched in the stomach by J. Gordon Whitehead, a McGill university student who was testing Houdini's well-known ability to withstand blows to the body. There is much speculation as to whether or not that punch may or may not have been the cause of Houdini's ruptured appendix.

In the "show must go on" tradition, the seriously ill Houdini continued his tour but eventually collapsed onstage in Detroit and was admitted to Grace Hospital suffering from peritonitis. Bess was also admitted to the hospital at the same time to be treated for her stomach ailments. Every day for nearly a week, she was wheeled into Houdini's room to visit with her husband. On October 31st, with his brother, Hardeen, at his side, Harry Houdini passed away. His last words were, "I'm tired of fighting."

After her husband's death, Bess continued to live in the Laurel Canyon house until the 1940s when her health began to deteriorate. After she moved away, the house was taken over by writer Lee Alden, who pioneered the women's movement and wrote *A Woman's Call to Arms* in 1950. People often referred to the author as the "Green Madonna" because whenever the moon was full, she would stand on one of the mansion's balconies wearing a green negligee and long green scarf (and nothing else) and allow the wind to blow through her hair and clothing. One day, for some unknown reason, she simply abandoned the house.

In 1959, a brush fire swept through Laurel Canyon destroying a number of the houses in the area. The Houdini mansion was one of them. What remained of the place was only the walls of the old building, the chauffeur's quarters and a portion of the garage. Today, nothing but ruins remain.

The ghost of Houdini does not rest in peace and he still walks the grounds where his beloved home once stood. Those who have come to the property, as many do on Halloween night, claim to have seen a dark figure standing on the staircases or walking in the garden grotto. Many believe that this is Houdini himself and that he comes back because he knows that the curse of the house contributed to his premature death.

Bessie Love's Haunted Cabin — 8227 Lookout Mountain Drive

Back in the mid 1800s, not long after California became a state, the Laurel Canyon area was a favorite hideout of the "Mexican Robin Hood," Tiburcio Vasquez, a bandit and folk hero who liked to steal from new landowners who were awarded the land that had been taken from the former Mexican farmers and ranchers. Vasquez would then hide his loot in nearby caves. His excuse for his crimes was alleged discrimination and being slighted by the *gringo norteamericanos* (Caucasian North Americans) and he held the belief that by acts of banditry, he might be able to regain California for his country of origin. At the time of Vasquez' birth, California was part of Mexico which lost the territory to the United States in the Mexican-American War in 1847.

Vasquez was well known for his crimes and when two fortune hunters got wind of the bandit's fortune, they came looking for the ill-gotten gold. Unfortunately for them, they were caught by Vasquez and killed on the land that actress Bessie Love's cabin would eventually be built.

Bessie Love was born Juanita Horton in Midland, Texas in 1898, but moved with her family to Hollywood when she was in the eighth grade. After her high school graduation, Bessie's mother sent her to the Biograph Studios in the hopes that she would become a star and could then help out the family financially. She met with producer D. W. Griffith who was enchanted by the young girl and he gave her a couple of small parts. By the time she was barely twenty years old, Bessie was making a great living in silent movies playing innocent young girls, flappers, and wholesome leading ladies.

In 1918, Love took some of her earnings and bought her first home, a lovely cabin in a beautifully rugged setting in the Hollywood Hills, but soon after she moved in, the actress discovered that she wasn't the only one living there. A variety of odd occurrences that she at first tried to ignore or explain away shattered the tranquility of her new home. She told friends that she would often hear a low moaning sound and men's voices when she was there alone. Then she began to experience electrical problems, had doors open and close by themselves, lights would turn themselves on and off, and there were definite cold spots felt in the living room, despite what the weather was like outside.

When one of Bessie's friends spent the night in a make-shift bed in the living room, she awoke to the sound of a man's voice. The living room was fully lit by the full moon, but she couldn't see anyone there. After hearing the voice again, she saw the figure of a transparent man walk through the living room wall right towards her. Then, after adjusting his cowboy hat, he continued through the living room and into the kitchen, not seeming to notice the terrified guest. The woman ran into Bessie's bedroom, where the two women stayed together for the rest of night.

Over the years, a number of people have made the cabin their home. In 1984, a new owner began a remodeling project, but that effort was quickly abandoned for some unknown reason. The cabin was vacant for nearly ten years, until a film electrician moved into the place in 1993.

During the week that he was moving in, he and his friend left the big, heavy wooden front door open out of necessity because it had a difficult lock that had to be turned in just the right manner. On one occasion, the heavy door slowly closed and locked itself, temporarily locking out the electrician. In another instance during that same week, the door once again slowly closed on its own and the dead bolt lock was also turned.

Once he moved in, the electrician experienced unexplainable electrical and power problems in the cabin which no one else in the community had experienced. Cold spots could be again felt in the living room and his fully charged cell phone wouldn't work as long as he was on the property, though in theory he was supposed to have cell coverage for that location.

Tiburcio Vaszuez was eventually arrested for his crimes and died by hanging on March 19, 1875, in San Jose, California. He is "honored" today by two places in Southern California that bear his name. Vasquez Canyon, the Big Tujunga tributary used by the outlaw in one of his famous getaways from the law, and Vasquez Rocks above Soledad Canyon, now a Los Angeles County park, which marks one of the bandito's favorite hideouts.

While Vasquez may very well have found peace in the afterlife, it is said that the ghosts of those two murdered fortune hunters still haunt the property and the cabin on Wonderland Avenue, looking for Vasquez's gold.

Errol Flynn's "House of Pleasure" — 3100 Torreyson Place

Errol Flynn designed and built his house in the Canyon in 1942 at a cost of $125,000 and turned the property into a fortress of "bacchanalian amusements." He even installed two-way mirrors in the ceilings of the bedrooms so that he and his friends could observe his famous house guests making love. Flynn, Hollywood's best known Casanova, once said of the home, "Strange people wended their way up the hill to the house. Among them pimps, sports, bums, down at the heels actors, queers, athletes, sightseers, process servers, phonies, salesmen — everything in the world."

The dashing movie hero whose winning smile and flashy swordplay made the ladies swoon had a reputation as a boozer, womanizer, and all-around bad boy. He was once quoted as saying, "It isn't what they say about you, it's what they whisper," and tongues were wagging in late 1942 when Errol was indicted by the Los Angeles County District Attorney's office on three charges of "statutory rape" for having sex with girls under the age of eighteen.

The girls, Betty Hansen and Peggy LaRue Satterlee claimed they had been seduced by the actor; once at the home of his friends, Bruce Cabot and Freddie McEvoy, and the other time on his boat, the *Sirocco*. If convicted, he could have spent twenty-five years in prison, but Flynn was eventually acquitted of the trumped-up charges. Those who knew him said he never fully recovered from the embarrassment and sniggering jokes that went with being tried for "rape" and by September 1959, it was clear to anyone who saw him that Errol had physically destroyed himself. Two doctors gave him just a year to live, but as it turned out, he left this world much sooner.

Flynn had come to Los Angeles to do some last-minute television work, an *Alcoa Presents* thirty-minute teleplay, *The Golden Shanty*, and then to guest on *The Red Skelton Show*. A couple of weeks later, he and his young "protégé" of the past two years, Beverly Aadland, flew to Vancouver, British Columbia, hoping to sell his beloved yacht *Zaca* to Canadian millionaire George Caldough. Errol badly needed money and might also have been trying to escape another charge of statutory rape in Los Angeles County because Beverly was barely seventeen years old.

Six days later, on October 14, Mr. and Mrs. Caldough were driving the couple to the Vancouver airport when Errol suddenly fell ill. On the Caldoughs' advice, they stopped at the apartment of Dr. Grant Gould, an old Flynn admirer. After holding court for several hours and treating one and all to his usual old Hollywood tales, Errol said he was tired and was taken to a bedroom to lie down. After about thirty minutes, Beverly looked in on him and found that the actor's face had turned blue and his lips were trembling. He seemed to be trying to speak but he could not get the words out. He died in her arms as she tried desperately to revive him.

Years of excessive living had taken their toll. Errol was barely fifty years old, but the coroner who later examined him said that his body was that of a man of seventy-five. As an homage to his hard-drinking lifestyle, Flynn was buried with six bottles of whiskey. His tell-all autobiography, *My Wicked Wicked Ways* was posthumously published a few months after his death.

In the years after his death, his old house became home to several famous names including actor Richard Dreyfuss, and singers Stuart Hamblin and Rick Nelson. This was Nelson's last home before his fatal plane crash in 1985. The house was torn down in June 1988, and all that's left is its foundation and a tennis court, but to this day, residents in neighboring homes have reported lights of all shapes and colors on the property and noises that sound like a social gathering or gala party going on. The most active month is usually August, when these noises are heard on almost a nightly basis.

The Hollywood Hills

The Hollywood Hills form the north barrier of the Los Angeles Basin. There has been extensive residential development in the Hollywood Hills since the 1920s, and the area is dotted with the mansions of the rich and famous. The hills are also marked by the tragic deaths of several of Hollywood's most well known players whose ghosts still like to make their presence known.

Inger Stevens

Actress Inger Stevens, best known for her portrayal as the Swedish housekeeper on the television show *The Farmer's Daughter* was an unhappy woman. Despite her success in Hollywood, her personal life was in a shambles. She was married to her agent, Anthony Soglio from 1955 to 1957, and it was rumored that she'd also had several less-than-satisfactory affairs with many Hollywood leading men, including Anthony Quinn. The actress attempted suicide once in 1959 when her reported romance with Bing Crosby came to an end. From 1961 until her death in 1970, she was secretly married to actor Ike Jones, but it's common knowledge that also she dated Burt Reynolds during the time she and Jones were married.

After *The Farmer's Daughter* was canceled in 1966, Inger concentrated on making movies such as *Hang 'Em High* with Clint Eastwood in 1968 and *Five Card Stud* with Dean Martin that same year. In early 1970, after concluding the filming of an ABC Television movie, *Run Simon Run*, Inger happily agreed to return to weekly television in a new series by producer Aaron Spelling, but on the morning of April 30th in 1970, she was found unconscious in the kitchen of her home at 8000 Woodrow Wilson Drive by a friend. The actress was rushed to a nearby hospital, but was declared dead on arrival at 10:30 a.m. She was only thirty-five years old.

An autopsy revealed that she died from an overdose of barbiturates, and while The Los Angeles County Coroner's office ruled her death as a suicide, many of Stevens' friends could not accept that notion. As always with apparent suicides, there is some speculation surrounding the circumstances, however, no foul play was ever proven in the Stevens case. The entry on her official Death Certificate states: "acute barbiturate intoxication due to ingestion of overdose".

Ike Jones stepped forward on the morning of the 30th and presented himself as Inger's husband so that he could claim the body. Her funeral and memorial service were held in private, with only a small number of family and friends in attendance. The actress was cremated and her ashes were scattered over the Pacific Ocean, but some say her unhappy spirit still haunts the house where she died.

Tallulah Bankhead

Actress Tallulah Bankhead was one of the most unique characters Hollywood has ever seen. According to those who knew her best, the actress was outspoken, uninhibited and outrageous despite her conservative Southern upbringing. Tallulah was born in 1902 in Huntsville, Alabama, to a prominent Alabama political family. Tallulah's grandfather, John Hollis Bankhead, was a Confederate veteran and a U.S. senator. Tallulah's Uncle John was also a senator and her father served as a U. S. Representative and Speaker of the House.

Tallulah discovered at an early age that theatrics were a viable outlet for gaining the attention she craved. She had a gift for mimicry and entertained her classmates by imitating their teachers. At the age of fifteen, Bankhead submitted her photo to *Picture Play* magazine which was conducting a contest and awarding a trip to New York plus a part in a movie to twelve lucky individuals solely based on their photographs. Tallulah learned that she was one of the winners while browsing through the magazine at a local drug store. She was ecstatic but both her father and grandmother had qualms about the young girl going to New York. William Bankhead soon realized, however, that there would be no peace for anyone until he gave Tallulah his consent.

She was paid $75 for three weeks work on *Who Loved Him Best* and though she only had a minor part, she quickly found her niche. But after five years of working in New York with no significant hits, she crossed the Atlantic and got her first big break on the London stage. Then, in 1930, Tallulah received a lucrative offer from Paramount Studios in Hollywood. She gave a huge party and reluctantly said farewell to England and sailed for New York in January of 1931.

Once she'd made her mark in Hollywood, Bankhead's escapades were on the tip of everybody's tongues. She reportedly engaged in hundreds of affairs with both men and women, and her biting wit, salty language, and outlandish behavior shocked and outraged everyone. It is said that she chain-smoked over one hundred cigarettes a day, drank gin and bourbon like they were water, and carried a suitcase-full of drugs to help her sleep, stay awake, and just function in general, but when Tallulah rented a house at 1712 North Stanley Avenue in Hollywood in 1931, she experienced something that might have driven her to drink had she not already have been so inclined.

While hosting a dinner party one evening for a group of friends, she looked up from the table to see the ghost of a horse appear in the room. "I was sitting there in bright light with six other people and I could see right through the horse," she claimed. "I saw it for about three seconds, and then it suddenly disappeared." Apparently nobody else in the room had witnessed the apparition, but when the actress told her neighbors about the strange sighting a few days later, they said that before she moved in, they had heard the sound of frightened horses in the area during a recent rainstorm.

Gia Scala

Actress Gia Scala made her motion picture debut in 1955 in *All That Heaven Allows* with Jane Wyman and Rock Hudson. She landed roles in *Tip On A Dead Jockey* and *The Garment Jungle* in 1957, and *The Tunnel of Love* in 1958. The latter featured Richard Widmark and Doris Day. Critics acclaimed Gia's performance as a labor organizer in *The Garment Jungle*, but personal problems plagued the actress. These problems drove her to an unsuccessful suicide attempt. After she recovered, the actress continued to work in both movies and television, but her career began to unravel as the result of a growing alcohol dependency. She was eventually let go from her studio contract and her marriage to stockbroker Donald Burnett ended in divorce. Being a British citizen she moved back to England, but once there her troubles only escalated. Suffering from severe emotional problems aggravated by alcohol, she made another unsuccessful suicide attempt before once again returning to Hollywood.

On the night of April 30, 1972, friends found the thirty-eight-year-old actress dead in her Hollywood Hills home at 7944 Woodrow Wilson Drive. She had apparently died from an overdose of drugs and alcohol. Police confirmed that she had been taking medication for a drinking problem.

While I couldn't find any reports stating that the Woodrow Wilson house is haunted, given the circumstances of her demise, one can't help but wonder whether or not she still might be lurking about.

Frank Christi

In 1982, actor and legendary tough guy Frank Christi, who appeared in the film *The Godfather* and the television shows *Charlie's Angels* and *The Rockford Files*, died screaming for mercy amid a hail of bullets in the carport of his home at 6969 Woodrow Wilson Drive. They say the out-of-work actor was killed by drug dealers, and even though the carport hasn't been reported as being actively haunted, a tragedy such as that leaves quite a bit of residual energy in its wake.

Larry Edmunds

Larry Edmunds Book Shop at 6644 Hollywood Boulevard has been selling books on the Boulevard since the 1930s. Although director Billy Wilder once said that Edmunds was a homosexual, Edmunds' business partner said Edmunds loved women and gave him the nickname of "Hollywood's greatest seducer."

Edmunds had great charm and was a hypnotic conversationalist. He became friends with John Barrymore, W. C. Fields, Marlene Dietrich, and writer Thomas Wolfe. It is said that he never stalked women — they stalked him. He reportedly seduced seventy-five percent of the secretaries in the studios as well as actresses Dolores Del Rio, Mary Astor, Margaret Sullivan, Paulette Goddard, Marlene Dietrich, Myrna Loy, Lupe Velez, and many others.

In 1940, Edmunds began to drink heavily. He was in and out of hospitals and sanitariums in an attempt to cope with his alcoholism. One day in 1941, when he had not shown up at the book store for two days, his partner went to Edmunds' home at 2472 Beachwood Canyon Drive where he found the thirty-five-year-old Edmunds lying dead on the kitchen floor. It appeared as though he had stuck his head in the gas oven. A suicide note explained the numerous holes in the nearby wall. The note said that he had made the holes with a knife, because he was "chopping off the heads of the little men that were creeping out of the wall." Realizing that he was that far gone, Edmonds decided to take his own life.

It is not known whether or not Larry haunts his old abode, but there are reports that his ghost is still seen on a regular basis at the book shop on Hollywood Boulevard.

Beverly Hills

The City of Beverly Hills was incorporated in 1914, and in 1915, the land was annexed to the city. Street lights and fire equipment were purchased and the tax rate was fixed at $1.00 for each $100.00 of assessed valuation.

In 1919, Douglas Fairbanks and Mary Pickford bought land on Summit Drive and built *Pickfair*, the house that would remain Pickford's home after she and Fairbanks divorced and for the rest of her life.

Other wealthy movie people soon followed suit and settled in Beverly Hills. Will Rogers, the wisecracking political humorist wrote about the land boom in 1923. "Lots are sold so quickly and often out here that they put through escrow made out to the twelfth owner... They couldn't possibly make out a separate deed for each purchaser; besides, he wouldn't have time to read it in the ten minutes' time he owned the land."

The movie colony was well entrenched by 1928 when Harold Lloyd built his mansion in Benedict Canyon, followed by John Barrymore, Robert Montgomery, and Miriam Hopkins. Thus, Beverly Hills became famous for being home to the rich and for the large, stylish mansions of famous movie stars.

While living in Beverly Hills was a dream come true to many, other residents left this world wishing that perhaps they had been living somewhere else.

Benjamin "Bugsy" Siegel

Notorious mobster Benjamin "Bugsy" Siegel was blown to bits in a gangland shooting while staying at the Beverly Hills home of his girlfriend, Virginia Hill in 1947. On the night of June 20, a mob hit-man, (allegedly Eddie Cannizzaro), hid outside the couple's mansion at 810 N. Linden Drive and shot Siegel several times with a U. S. military M1 Carbine as he sat near a window reading the *Los Angeles Times*. One of the .30-caliber bullets smashed the bridge of Siegel's nose, and the impact blew Siegel's left eyeball out of its socket. It was found intact, fourteen feet away from the body. The coroner's autopsy report states that Siegel died instantly of a cerebral hemorrhage due to gunshot wounds to the head. Amongst his possessions at the time of the murder were a billfold containing $408 in cash, a watch, a money clip, a key chain with six keys on it, one being a hotel room key, a ring, and a pair of cufflinks.

The crime remains technically unsolved since no one was ever charged with this bloody and much-photographed mob murder, but Hollywood historian Scott Michaels recalls reading an article in the *Los Angeles Times* several years ago about a writer who was approached by an ex-gangster named Eddie Cannizzaro. Cannizzaro wanted to earn a few quick bucks by selling his story to the writer. The writer wasn't too impressed until Eddie told him that he would reveal that he was the one who killed "Bugsy" Siegel. That got the writer's attention, but when he mentioned to Eddie that there is no statute of limitations for murder, Cannizzaro quickly clammed up. They say the next time Eddie ever opened his mouth again about being the hit man who whacked Siegel was on his deathbed in 1987.

Psychics have reported seeing the spirit of "Bugsy" Siegel cowering in fear amid a hail of phantom bullets, reliving his final moments on earth over and over again. The house still stands but the current owners don't seem to be bothered by the mobster's spirit. Maybe that's because Siegel seems to travel around quite a bit, most probably to get away from the scene of the crime. His ghost has been seen lurking around the Flamingo Hotel in Las Vegas, dressed in a smoking jacket and grinning from ear to ear. He has also been seen in the presidential suite at the hotel which was his home for many years, and he also pops up in and around the rose garden or in the wedding chapel area.

Lupe Velez

Actress Lupe Velez, also known as "Whoopee Lupe" and "The Mexican Spitfire," had a short but successful Hollywood career and a long line of famous boyfriends to go along with it. At one time or another she was linked to Charlie Chaplin, Gary Cooper, Jimmy Durante, Douglas Fairbanks, Sr., and Anthony Quinn. She was also married to actor Johnny Weismuller of *Tarzan* fame from 1933-1939. Regarding her long list of beaus, she was once quoted as saying, "The first time you buy a house you see how pretty the paint is and buy it. The second time you look to see if the basement has termites. It's the same with men."

In the mid-1940s Lupe was involved in a relationship with a married actor, Harald Maresch, and became pregnant with his child. Maresch would not leave his wife, and Lupe, following her strict Catholic upbringing, refused to have an abortion. Unable to face the shame of giving birth to an illegitimate child, the actress decided to take her own life. On the evening of December 13, 1944, she retired to bed after taking an overdose of secobarbital, but instead of sending her to sleep, the drug upset her stomach, and she was found dead in her bathroom, reportedly with her head in the toilet bowl.

Another gentler version of the story claims that the actress wrote several suicide notes, then swallowed a full bottle of seconal tablets and was found dead the next morning in her bed with its white silk sheets and pillow cases. Dressed in blue satin pajamas, she was lying as if asleep under an eiderdown quilt. Lupe's suicide note read, "To Harald, may God forgive you and forgive me too but I prefer to take my life away and our baby's before I bring him with shame or killing him, Lupe." Her body was returned to her homeland of Mexico for burial, but some say her ghost has stayed behind at the house at 732 N. Rodeo Drive.

Rudolph Valentino

Falcon Lair at 1436 Bella Drive is haunted by one of the most well-traveled ghosts in Hollywood, Rudolph Valentino. His spirit has been seen at Hollywood Forever Cemetery where he is buried, at Paramount Studios, and at his beloved Falcon Lair. Actor Harry Carey was one of several subsequent owners who has seen the dead actor's ghost. Actress Millicent Rogers reportedly spent only one night in the house before being chased out by Valentino's specter.

His apparition has been seen in his old bedroom, in the darkened corridors and at the stables where he kept his beloved horse. One stable worker abruptly quit after seeing Valentino's ghost petting the horse. Passersby have reported seeing Valentino's dark silhouette looking out over the LA skyline from his favorite window on the second floor.

George Reeves

The ghost of TV's *Superman*, actor George Reeves, has been frequently seen in the house where he died in 1959.

Whether it was murder or suicide, nobody knows, and because Reeves' body was exhumed and cremated in 1961, the cause of his death will forever remain a mystery. But what *is* known is that his ghost refuses to leave the house where he died. Several people who have lived in the house in recent years have moved out because of the unsettling ghostly incidents they have experienced there.

A single gunshot is often heard in the bedroom where he died and inexplicable noises can be heard in the bedroom as well. Lights turn on and off by themselves, and Reeves' ghost has appeared to several people, dressed in his Superman costume. Neighbors have even reported seeing his apparition on the front lawn. Singer Don McLean (*American Pie*) recorded a song called "Superman's Ghost," as a tribute to George Reeves and the troubles he had with being typecast in his "Man of Steel" role. The house is located at 1759 Benedict Canyon Drive.

Haunted Intersections

S ometimes just driving around Hollywood and doing
a little sightseeing can result in an inadvertent ghost
sighting or two, especially if you happen upon one of
our city's most famously haunted intersections.

Laurel Canyon Boulevard and Lookout Mountain Drive

In 1913, the nation's first trackless trolley was installed
to bring residents and prospective buyers from the streetcar
line at Sunset Boulevard to a roadhouse tavern at Lookout
Mountain Avenue in Laurel Canyon. The fare was just ten
cents, but the trolley was retired after only five years as canyon transportation was quickly replaced by Stanley Steamers
and then by the automobile. With cars came the paved roads
that grew throughout
the subdivided canyon
properties. But these
days, at the intersec-
tion of Laurel Canyon
Boulevard and Look-
out Mountain Drive,
unwary drivers some-
times get a dangerous
glimpse of what life
was like in the canyon
long before the cars
and trolleys.

Many people claim to have witnessed the apparition of a vintage carriage pulled by white horses that comes charging out of the road from Lookout Mountain. The horses appear to be galloping at full speed, and many an unwary driver has crashed his automobile trying frantically to get out of the way, only to have the horse and carriage disappear right before their eyes just seconds before impact.

Hollywood Boulevard and Sierra Bonita Avenue
The legend of Cowboys and Indians has been portrayed in Hollywood films since movies came to Hollywood, but Indians were here long before the advent of shoot-em-up Westerns or the arrival of the white man.

In pre-Spanish days, the area now called Los Angeles, was inhabited by approximately 4,000 Indians representing some 30 tribes. It all started around 8,000 BC when the Chumash people settled in the Los Angeles Basin. By 500 AD, the Tongva Indians inhabited Los Angeles, and according to some accounts, they displaced the Chumash. The Yang-Na Indians settled by the Los Angeles River and the Indian village of Yangna eventually became the city of Los Angeles. It is believed that the Tongva lived at the base of the canyons and that a community of more than 200 Native Americans lived at the junction of Franklin and Coldwater canyons. This gave them yearlong access to fresh flowing water without being too far from the marshy flood plain; the vast cienegas that filled the flatland between Baldwin Hills and Beverly Hills. These marshes, which were navigated in reed canoes, contained a rich supply of the plants and animals that sustained them.

While the Indian culture has long since vanished, there seems to be a residual haunting at the corner of Sierra Bonita Avenue and Hollywood Boulevard. Pedestrians and motorists alike have reported seeing a wide variety of pioneer-era apparitions. Indians on foot and horseback are most frequently observed, but flying tomahawks and arrows have also been seen. One driver reportedly ran into a tree when he swerved to avoid the specter of a covered wagon crossing the intersection. With all this urban revitalization of Indian land, is it any wonder that a few phantom tomahawks and arrows shatter the tranquility of an otherwise peaceful neighborhood from time to time?

Hollywood Boulevard and Cahuenga

On August 5, 1994, the Los Angeles City Council officially designated the corner of Hollywood and Cahuenga Boulevards "Raymond Chandler Square." Proposed by journalist Jess Bravin, the U. S. Supreme Court reporter for the Wall Street Journal who conceived the monument as a way for the city to honor the man who, in Bravin's words, "all but invented our city's literary landscape," Chandler Square is dedicated to writer Raymond Chandler (1888-1959) who shaped the image of Los Angeles through his gritty crime stories and novels, including *The Big Sleep* and *Farewell, My Lovely*. The author's most famous character, Philip Marlowe, has become synonymous with the tradition of the hard-boiled private detective. The corner of Hollywood and Cahuenga was made famous by Marlowe, because in the novels, Marlowe's office was in the "Cahuenga Building" which was actually the Pacific Security Bank Building.

In addition to the many tourists who visit the historic marker daily, several ghosts are said to haunt Chandler Square as well. Raymond Chandler died of pneumonia at the Scripps Clinic in La Jolla, California on March 26, 1959, but one can't help but wonder if he might be one of them.

Hollywood and Vine

This well-known intersection became famous in the 1920s for its concentration of radio and movie related businesses when, during the Golden Age of Hollywood, the area began to see an influx of money and influence as movie and music businesses began to move in. In urban folklore, many of the local buildings are considered to be part of Haunted Hollywood, home to the ghosts of celebrities (and a few less stellar residents) of Hollywood's legendary past. On May 29, 2003, Hollywood and Vine was named "Bob Hope Square" to commemorate Hope's 100th birthday, and it is at this famous intersection where stories of two separate hauntings live on. Not surprisingly, both the ghosts belong to legendary horror movie stars.

Actor Lon Chaney was one of the greatest horror stars of all time and is probably best remembered for his characterizations of tortured, often grotesque and afflicted characters, as well as his groundbreaking artistry with film makeup, as evidenced in the original *Phantom of the Opera*. The departed actor's ghost was often seen sitting on a bus bench at the southeast corner of Hollywood and Vine, right in front of the famous Taft Building which once housed offices for Charlie Chaplin and Will Rogers, and, from 1935 to 1945, the Academy of Motion Picture Arts and Sciences. Built in 1923, it was the first building on the Boulevard built to the maximum 150 foot height limit.

Although reports of Chaney's ghost ceased when the bench was removed a few years ago, one can't help but wonder if Chaney's ghost still comes by from time to time, hoping to find his beloved bench reinstalled.

It's said that another horror star, Bela Lugosi, who will be forever known as the sinister vampire Count Dracula, is still seen taking a walk past the famous intersection; a daily ritual he undertook when he was alive.

Lugosi lived not far away in a small apartment on Harold Way during his final years. When he died on August 16,

1956, from years of addiction to morphine, Demerol, and other drugs he used to combat the effects of a war injury, his body was sent over to the Utter-McKinley Mortuary at 6240 Hollywood Boulevard just a block east of Vine Street. It was a familiar place to the famous actor because he would often stop in during his daily walks and chat with the receptionist. Given the number of famous stars who made Utter-McKinley their last stop on the way to the cemetery, there is no doubt that Bela had also been there paying his last respects many times.

In Vincent Price's autobiography, he tells the story of visiting the mortuary with Peter Lorre after Lugosi's death to pay their respects. As they were standing in front of the casket viewing Lugosi's body, Lorre turned to Price and asked, "Should we drive a stake through his heart, just in case?" Who says horror stars don't have a sense of humor?

It was Lugosi's wish that he be buried in his Dracula cape and hundreds of fans lined Hollywood Boulevard to view Lugosi's body, but it seems that the actor's restless spirit just couldn't resist visiting one of his favorite haunts one last time.

The mortuary had made agreements with the Hollywood Chamber of Commerce that Lugosi's funeral procession would not travel down Hollywood Boulevard on the way to the Holy Cross Cemetery in Culver City. For some reason, they thought that the sight of Lugosi's hearse might be bad for business, but apparently Bela's ghost thought differently. As the hearse pulled out of the mortuary, the driver's intention was to head north and cross Hollywood Boulevard, but suddenly, he seemed to lose control of the vehicle and veered to the left, turned onto the street, and the driver was unable to regain control of the hearse until after it crossed Hollywood and Vine.

The Paramount Studios & Hollywood Forever Cemetery Connection

Paramount Pictures Corporation has been in existence for more than ninety-five years, making it the longest-lived American movie studio ever. Its beginnings date back to May, 1912, with the formation of the Famous Players Film Company founded by Adolph Zukor, the owner of a New York nickelodeon after Zukor secured American distribution rights to Sarah Bernhart's four-reel film, *Queen Elizabeth*. The film's triumphant opening on July 12, 1912 as the first full length drama shown in the United States prompted Zukor to found the Famous Players Film Company which began to produce movies in New York beginning with *The Prisoner of Zenda* and *The Count of Monte Carlo*.

That same year, another aspiring producer, Jesse L. Lasky opened the Lasky Feature Play Company with money borrowed from his brother-in-law, Samuel Goldfish (later to be known as Samuel Goldwyn). As their first employee, the Lasky company hired a stage director with no film experience, Cecil B. DeMille, who would find a suitable location site in Hollywood, near Los Angeles, for his first film, *The Squaw Man*.

Beginning in 1914, both Lasky and Famous Players released their films through a startup company, Paramount Pictures. Organized early that year by a Utah theater owner, W. W. Hodkinson, who had bought and merged several smaller firms, Paramount was the first successful nationwide distributor. Until this time films had been sold on a statewide or regional basis.

Soon after, the ambitious Zukor, who was not used to taking a secondary role, began courting Hodkinson and Lasky, and in 1916, Zukor maneuvered a three-way merger of his Famous Players, the Lasky company, and Paramount. The new company, Famous Players-Lasky, grew quickly with Lasky and his partners, Goldfish and DeMille, running the production side, Hiram Abrams in charge of distribution, and Zukor making great plans. With only the exhibitor-owned First National as a rival, Famous Players-Lasky and its "Paramount Pictures" soon dominated the business.

Hollywood Forever Cemetery has been in the neighborhood a bit longer than Paramount. It was founded as Hollywood Memorial Park Cemetery in 1899 by Hollywood denizens I. N. Van Nuys and Colonel Isaac Lankershim on one hundred prime acres in the heart of Hollywood. In 1901, Mrs. Highland Price, a blacksmith's wife, was the first person to be interred at the cemetery. Since then, some of the most famous stars in the history of Hollywood, including Rudolph Valentino, Douglas Fairbanks, Nelson Eddy, Peter Lorre, Janet Gaynor, Tyrone Power, and Clifton Webb have been laid to rest at Hollywood Forever. Many other famous Los Angelinos are buried at the cemetery as well. They include, Harrison Gray Otis, longtime publisher of the *Los Angeles Times*, Col. Griffith J. Griffith, who gave Griffith Park and Griffith Observatory to the city of Los Angeles, Senator Cornelius Cole, and Hollywood pioneer John T. Gower.

By the late 1990s, the cemetery had fallen into disrepair and was on the verge of being closed for good thanks to the mishandling of funds by owner Jules Roth.

Roth, a convicted felon who had served five years in San Quentin for grand theft and securities fraud, bought the cemetery in the late 1930s, and over the years, stole millions of dollars in cemetery revenue. It wasn't until the 1980s that officials began raising questions, and state regulators eventually seized the property in 1995. Roth was being investigated by the city state's attorney when he died of pneumonia in January 1998.

By then, Hollywood Memorial Park's threatened closure was imminent. At the eleventh hour, an enterprising young man from St. Louis named Tyler Cassity, who's family was in the cemetery business, stepped in and bought the crumbling ruins for a mere $375,000 at auction. At the time of purchase, it was estimated that it would cost Cassity another $7 million to refurbish the place, but he did the work. In the process, he not only changed the cemetery name to Hollywood Forever, he launched it into the twenty-first century with amenities such as a funeral chapel equipped for live worldwide webcasts of funeral services for those who cannot attend in person and computerized kiosks scattered around the property where people can go and look up the life stories of many of the cemetery's permanent residents.

The Hollywood Forever/Paramount Studios connection begins with a common wall separating the two properties. Not surprisingly, many of the stars and employees who worked for Paramount are buried in Hollywood Forever. The adjoining wall is located closest to Stages 29 through 32, and many people have reported seeing spirits walking directly through the wall from one lot to the next. Those who have witnessed these apparitions claim that the ghosts often are dressed in clothing from the 1930s and 40s.

Out of all of the sound stages in that area, Stages 31 and 32 seem to have the most ghostly activity. Footsteps are often heard tapping through stages that have been secured for the night, and it is not uncommon for equipment to turn on and off and operate by itself.

The studio's large stage doors make a very loud sound when they are opened or shut and there is no way to muffle the sound of a door closing. When someone enters or leaves, it is plainly heard. One evening, three guards secured Stage 32 for the night. One of the men had gone outside and closed and locked the door securely behind him. The remaining two guards were looking around the place, making sure that everything was in order, when they suddenly heard someone walking behind one of the stage flats. They walked over and looked behind the partition, but no one was there. Moments later, they heard the stage door being opened. Puzzled, but convinced that it was the third guard, they secured the rest of the stage and left to find the third member of the team sitting outside. He had not entered the sound stage.

Another guard had a more frightening experience on this same stage. He was working by himself and shortly after finishing his rounds for the night, he turned off the lights, and just as he was leaving, he heard someone walking across the stage. He wondered how anyone could see to walk around in the darkness on a stage that was filled with props and scenery for the next day's filming. It was difficult enough to move around when the lights were on.

Somehow though, the footsteps continued, crossing the darkened stage unobstructed. The startled guard turned on his flashlight and checked out the sound, but no one was there. After that incident, he never closed down that stage by himself again.

Paramount Studios has many entrances and some of them are walk-in gates, like the one at Lemon Grove Avenue, just a few feet from the cemetery. It is here where many of the ghosts from the graveyard are also said to enter the studio lot. According to guards posted there, some spirits actually appear as heads that poke through the cemetery wall and then disappear. Others actually walk through the gate itself, like the ghost of silent film heartthrob Rudolph Valentino. But Valentino is just one of many Hollywood Forever ghosts who sometimes appear at the gates. This does not please the security guards at all, especially those who work the night shift.

Most of the guards know everyone who comes in an out of the gates because they see them every day. One evening, the night shift guard noticed an unfamiliar face lurking about. He followed the man to a corner of the wall leading into the cemetery, and thinking he had him cornered, waited for the suspicious visitor to come out. After a minute or two, he looked around the corner just in time to see the man vanish right through the cemetery wall. From that time on, he refused to work the Lemon Grove gate at night.

Hollywood Forever is home to a number of hauntings as well.

Virginia Rappe and "Fatty" Arbuckle

Virginia Rappe was a popular young starlet from 1916 until her untimely death in 1921. She also has the distinction of being the center of the biggest scandal to ever rock Hollywood during that era. Although she was ultimately discovered to have died of peritonitis caused by a ruptured bladder, it was initially allegedly that she had been raped by silent screen comic Roscoe "Fatty" Arbuckle during a wild party at the Saint Francis Hotel in San Francisco.

Arbuckle was accused of her rape and murder and brought to trial. Although he was ultimately acquitted after enduring three manslaughter trials, the scandal ruined both Arbuckle's motion picture career and his life. He turned to alcohol to help ease the pain. His career was eventually resurrected in 1929, when he signed a contract with Jack Warner to star in six two-reel Vitaphone short comedies under his own name.

The six Vitaphone shorts filmed in Brooklyn constitute the only recordings of the actor's voice. Silent-film comedian Al St. John (Arbuckle's nephew) as well as actors Lionel Stander and Shemp Howard (of The Three Stooges fame) appeared with Arbuckle in the shorts. After he had finished filming the last of the two-reelers on June 28, 1933, Arbuckle was signed by Warner Brothers to make a feature-length film. Finally, his professional reputation was restored, and "Fatty" would at last be returning to the world he loved.

Arbuckle was elated, and right after he signed the contract, he was quoted as saying, "This is the best day of my life." But the exhilaration may have been too much for the rotund actor, because he died that night of congestive heart failure at the age of forty-six. Although some might consider Arbuckle's early passing a tragedy, it seems as though that wasn't enough to satisfy the scorned ghost of Virginia Rappe. Whether it's because of the verdict that set the actor free, or that she is simply bemoaning the fact that she died at such an early age, she has been seen on numerous occasions kneeling in front of her gravestone and wailing loudly into the night.

Clifton Webb

The ghost of actor Clifton Webb, who is probably best known for his role as *Mr. Belvedere,* is another spirit who roams the cemetery. Webb can often be seen strolling along the corridors of the Abbey of the Psalms mausoleum where he is buried alongside his mother.

Psychic to the Stars Kenny Kingston and Mr. Webb were good friends in life and continue to be so even though Mr. Webb is now in the afterlife. I spoke to Kenny some time ago when I was writing a magazine article on the cemetery and its resident ghosts and asked him why the actor continues to haunt the mausoleum. "Clifton refuses to accept the fact that he's dead," Kenny explained. "He often visits his home on Rexford Drive but prefers staying close to the cemetery." Kenny also added that Mr. Webb is not the least bit shy about having people see his apparition, which may account for the numerous sightings.

Ditra Flame, Rudolph Valentino, and "Bugsy" Siegel

Another ghost who is regularly seen in the cemetery is referred to as *The Lady in Black* who visits Rudolph Valentino's crypt on a regular basis. There are lots of theories about who she might be, but from the first day of Valentino's entombment, this "Lady in Black" would walk through the cemetery, into the main building, directly to Valentino's tomb, place red roses in the flower holders, then rub her glove-covered hand over his name and date of birth and death, making certain it was clear of dust and finger prints and then kneel before his tomb and pray.

The original Lady in Black reportedly was a woman named Ditra Flame. As a child she had become very sick and was put in the hospital. Rudolph, a friend of her mother, is said to have come to her bedside, and put a rose on her bed, supposedly saying, "...if I die before you do, you please come and stay by me because I don't want to be alone either. You come and talk to me."

Ditra got better, and when Valentino died on August 23, 1926, at the age of thirty-one, she brought a bouquet of red roses to Rudy's crypt every year up until 1955. According to many, even now, after her death, she continues to pay tribute to Valentino.

Valentino's ghost has also been known to take a nightly stroll through the cemetery grounds and so has the spirit of legendary gangster Benjamin Siegelbaum or, as he's better known, "Bugsy" Siegel, who is buried in the Beth Olam section of the cemetery. He picked up the loathsome nickname "Bugsy," early in his career because of his reputation for being a hothead who "went bugs" quite easily. It's interesting to note that the marker on Siegel's crypt reads: "In Loving Memory From The Family." One can only imagine which "family" it is referring to.

George Harrison and Mama Cass Elliot

Hollywood Forever also played a role in the final disposition of former Beatle George Harrison. In keeping with his Eastern faith, just hours after he passed away at a friend's Hollywood Hills home, the family had his body cremated by Hollywood Forever. His ashes were then returned to the family, and were said to have been scattered in the sacred Ganges River in India, but the actual disposition of his ashes has not been publicly disclosed. While there have been no reported sightings of Harrison's ghost mingling with many of the other celebrities interred at the cemetery, it could be that he and Mama Cass Elliot, who was cremated at Hollywood Forever in 1978, understand that the place of their cremations was merely a stopping off point on the way to the big jam session in the sky and don't care to stick around.

Jules Roth

And finally, despite all his dastardly wrong doings when he was the owner of Hollywood Forever, Jules Roth, who died at the age of ninety-eight in 1998, is buried there and lies in a crypt inside the cemetery's Cathedral Mausoleum just below the final resting place of his parents. To date, nobody has seen his tall, lanky apparition roaming about, but a likeness of him in the form of a bronze bust, which the vain Roth had commissioned years ago, now resides in Tyler Cassity's office.

Not long after Cassity settled into his new job, he made an amazing discovery in a Westside junk shop when he came face-to-face with an exquisitely sculpted bronze bust of the man whose cemetery he had just bought. It had been hauled off along with everything else of value in Roth's Hollywood Hills home and sold at auction to help satisfy Roth's personal debts, which were many. In fact, there wasn't even enough money in Roth's estate to cover his death expenses. On the rainy afternoon when Roth's body was transported from a funeral home across the street to the cemetery, instead of his casket being transported by the customary hearse, it was unceremoniously thrown onto the back of a pickup truck.

Paramount Studios is located at 5555 Melrose Avenue, Hollywood, California 90038. The entrance to the Hollywood Forever Cemetery is at 6000 Santa Monica Boulevard, Hollywood, California 90038.

MEET ME AT   WHERE THE
THE FORMOSA   STARS DINE

The Formosa Café

7156 Santa Monica Boulevard
West Hollywood, California 90046

The Formosa Café, has been (and continues to be) a popular hangout for nearly every movie star in Hollywood, as evidenced by the sign that hangs over the bar which reads: "Where the Stars Dine."

The restaurant's walls are lined with over 250 black and white photos of celebrities who frequented the establishment in the past and present and over the years, the likes of James Dean, Humphrey Bogart, Elvis Presley, Marilyn Monroe, Marlon Brando, Jack Benny, and Grace Kelly have all either rubbed elbows at the bar or slid into one of the Formosa's cushy red leather booths to enjoy the yummy Asian cuisine.

The café has been featured in several motion pictures. In the 1997 film noir, *L.A. Confidential*, you may recognize The Formosa as the dark restaurant where a detective mistakes the real Lana Turner for a hooker. In reality, Lana Turner and her gangster boyfriend, Johnny Stompanato, were regulars back in the 50s before Lana's daughter stabbed Stompanato to death in self-defense. Johnny's associates in crime, gangsters Mickey Cohen and "Bugsy" Siegel were also café regulars.

In the 1920s, the building was used as a production office for the historic Warner Hollywood Studios which is just across the street. In 1939, an enterprising man by the name of Lem Quon, along with his partner, Jim Bernstein, transformed the property into The Formosa Café. Bernstein was a friend of mobster Mickey Cohen who ran a bookie operation out of the restaurant, and to this day you can see Cohen's floor safe next to one of the booths. The trendy eatery/bar has been run by Quon's family all these years, and Vince Jung, Quon's grandson is the current owner.

Vince has worked at the restaurant most of his life and took over the helm shortly after his grandfather Lem passed away. As a child, Vince used to come in after school to do his homework in one of the back booths and has met many celebrities over the years. "I was just a kid when I met John Wayne," Vince recalls. "He was a mammoth of a man."

According to legend, Wayne, who was a Formosa regular, once passed out in his favorite booth after a hard night of drinking. At closing time, the bartender called Vince's dad, who then ran the place, to find out whether or not he should try and wake the sleeping giant. Mr. Jung said, "I've got to open up tomorrow at 7:00 AM anyway, so go ahead a let him sleep it off."

Apparently Wayne felt very much at home at The Formosa because when Mr. Jung showed up the next morning to open up, the first thing he heard was Wayne calling out to him from the kitchen asking how he'd like his eggs.

Today, The Formosa continues to be a popular industry watering hole, especially after dark. To the naked eye, not much about the place has changed since 1939 and Vince likes to say that The Formosa is Hollywood's version of *Cheers*. "Most of the people who come here are regulars," says Vince, "but we also get our fair share of celebrities. Not long ago I came downstairs and there was James Gandolfini, Pamela Anderson, and Sasha Baron Cohen sitting at the bar with their own groups of friends, all on the same night."

While there haven't been any reported sightings of any celebrity ghosts at the restaurant, its former owner and several other ghostly patrons from the past still drop by from time to time to clandestinely mingle with the likes of Bono, Michael Douglas, and Christian Slater. Although Vince himself has not witnessed anything paranormal, he's constantly hearing stories from his employees who have.

Juan Aviles, who has worked at The Formosa for eight years, says most of the restaurant's spirits aren't particularly scary, although the shadows he frequently sees sometimes do make him a little nervous. It is his theory that the more jittery they make him, the stronger they seem to get and they seem to feed off his fright. His way of dealing with it is by asking them not to scare him, but every so often they still do.

"I was in the kitchen by myself one day when someone called out my name," Aviles recalls. "I thought it might have been my boss, but when I went to check, there was nobody there. This has happened three times so far."

Another time he was closing up and was just about to leave the building when he heard what sounded like someone grabbing a bunch of silverware and jingling it around. "I've been here long enough to recognize the normal sounds of this place, and that wasn't normal. Whoever it was wanted to get my attention, and did."

Chef Owen Timoteo has been the cook at The Formosa for about six months. He claims that when he used to work alone on the weekends he'd hear strange noises, hear voices, and see white shadows go past him which, at first, he dismissed as nothing. It wasn't until he and another cook were in the kitchen and saw a pot on the stove lift itself up and then set itself back down a few inches away that he finally convinced himself that the restaurant was indeed haunted.

"I've had several other experiences since that one," he says. "One day I walked out into the bar area and was looking into the mirror over the bar and I saw someone sitting in one of the booths, but when I turned around to see who it was, there was nobody there."

Not long after that, he was in the kitchen and heard what sounded like someone dropping something heavy on one of the tables in the other room. Thinking it might be Vince bringing in a bag of groceries, he called out, but nobody answered, so he called Vince on the phone to see if he might be upstairs in the office. He was dismayed to find out that Vince was at home and nobody else was in the restaurant. "That was the last time I ever worked alone here," says Owen. "I don't want to see or hear anything like that again, although I hear noises all the time. And when I'm working in the kitchen, I always feel as though there's someone standing behind me."

With so much ghostly activity reported at The Formosa, I had to go and investigate, and I invited paranormal investigators Victoria Gross and Barry Conrad to join me. After doing a quick walk thru of the restaurant, Victoria, a psychic medium, had to agree with Owen that the restaurant was indeed quite haunted.

As soon as she ventured into the kitchen, Victoria immediately picked up on the spirit of a man. "There's a very strong, aggressive energy over by the stove," she told us after her initial investigation. "It was like he was warning me that this is his domain and I wasn't supposed to be in here. He's a very old spirit, a very protective Asian man, probably a cook, and he let me know that he did not want me in his space. He's very serious and took a lot of pride in his work. I saw him as being about 45-50 years old, and he dates back to the 1930s or 40s. He's rather short and kind of stocky in stature and was wielding a cleaver in his hand. He doesn't want to leave here and I get the feeling that he's overseeing everything that goes on."

While Victoria was in the kitchen doing her investigation, Vince and I were at the bar talking about his grandfather, Lem, who worked at the restaurant for fifty-three years. "He loved this place; it was pretty much his life and he did everything

Psychic investigators Barry Conrad and Victoria Gross.

here," said Vince. "He loved being around people, especially celebrities and enjoyed that facet of the business. He always had a keen understanding that no matter what type of clientele we have, we're in the hospitality business and the rest is just icing on the cake. People would come in just to hang out with him."

When Victoria and I compared notes later on, her description of the man in the kitchen perfectly matched Vince's description of his grandfather, who did, in fact, do most of the cooking for many years.

The Formosa was Lem Quon's second home, and he worked there until the last day of his life. According to Vince, his grandfather had not been feeling good that particular Sunday, but stayed at work until about one in the morning. He passed away at the age of eighty-four just a few hours after he arrived home, but Lem is still around, in spirit, making sure that his beloved restaurant runs smoothly...and he's not above taking matters into his own hands when need be.

A former chef was out in the dining room taking a break and was standing next to "Lem's booth" when all of a sudden, he got pinched by unseen hands. (Apparently Lem used to pinch his employees to get them moving when they seemed to be lazing around.) The poor chef got so upset he started yelling, "Lem pinched me! Lem pinched me!" and needless to say, he caused quite a stir.

"It might have been my grandfather who did that," laughed Vince, "because the guy shouldn't have been in the dining room to begin with."

The Trolly
One of the most charming aspects of The Formosa is it's famed trolley car, a relic from a time in Los Angeles history when streetcars were the city's only form of public transportation. The trolleys ran the city streets from Downtown to

Hollywood and East Los Angeles from the 1880s and to the 1950s. The Formosa trolley which was built in 1896 was one of the original Pacific Railways cars that ran down Santa Monica Boulevard and was added to the restaurant in 1945.

"The car was slated for demolition," said Vince, "and we needed to expand, so we not only saved the car, but saved ourselves construction costs as well by just attaching it to the building for additional seating."

When Victoria walked into the quaint trolley car section of the restaurant she immediately picked up the spirit of a tall, jolly man from the 1940s or 50s who gave her the name *Harold*. "He was not a movie star," she said, "but more like a producer-type. She went on to explain that she got the impression that this ghost was quite active and frequently came to visit because this was one of his favorite places to be when he was alive. "He loves to watch people and comes to have fun, like playing little pranks on the customers," she told us. "I get the impression that things move around in here quite a bit or just seem to disappear."

Vince and I were standing just a few feet away from Victoria while she was communicating with Harold, chatting quietly amongst ourselves. Things seemed to be going smoothly for Victoria until I happened to ask Vince whether or not there had been any murders or deaths at the restaurant. As he started telling me about a shooting that took place many years ago, Victoria noticed that Harold's energy quickly changed from lighthearted to dour and then he simply faded away. "He was here and witnessed the shooting in the spirit realm," she explained, "and didn't like what he saw."

Another entity in the trolley car is that of a young man who seemed to be quite frustrated. "It's like he's waiting for someone, but I can't tell whether or not he is waiting in spirit, or if this occurred when he was alive," Victoria explained. "He's just sitting here watching people pass him by, but it's like nobody sees him and he's angry about it. He says his name is John and he's telling me that he feels trapped, but I don't feel like he's trapped at all because he doesn't want me to help him cross over. I also sense that he doesn't have any ties to the restaurant and actually spends most of his time outside on the street and just pops in every so often when he's attracted by someone in the restaurant who is sensitive to his psychic energy."

It soon became apparent that John was thriving on all of our psychic energy because he quickly made an attempt to try and take over Victoria's body. Victoria felt quite dizzy and a bit disoriented. It took everything she had to get him to back off a bit.

It was then that she decided it was best that we all move away from the trolley and back out into the bar where Victoria encountered three more ghosts. One was the spirit of a little girl, running playfully up and down the aisle, another was a sad woman spirit sitting at the bar, and finally, a playful male spirit who, like Harold, enjoyed making things move around. Victoria thought that he might be the one responsible for some of the strange noises employees report hearing after the restaurant is closed.

Victoria says that there is nothing particularly threatening about the ghosts she encountered at The Formosa, even if they do like to make their presence known from time to time. It also seems like they are there to keep the restaurant safe because The Formosa's existence has been endangered a number of times, most recently in the 1989 when it was threatened with demolition when its lease expired. Fortunately, there was such a furor about turning the historic site into a parking lot that news of The Formosa's imminent destruction spread like wildfire. "The news of this little mom and pop restaurant even made CNN," says Vince. "What does that tell you?"

Thanks to concerted citizens and preservationist efforts the restaurant was not only preserved in its present location but also designated as a historic landmark. While Vince is happy that so many people stepped in to save The Formosa, he also thinks that the restaurant itself (and possibly the spirits within) had something to do with keeping it from the wrecking ball. "The place has always had it's own weird energy," he explained, "and has always found a way to survive."

The Magic Castle

7001 Franklin Avenue, Hollywood, California 90068

The Magic Castle is not only a Hollywood landmark and well-known performance venue for the magic industry, it is one of the most famous magic clubs in the world. Because it is a private club, you must be a member or have a guest card from a member to get in unless you happen to visit in spirit or happen to be one of the castle's resident ghosts.

The castle was once a beautiful Victorian home built in 1909 by real estate magnate Rollin B. Lane. The Lane home was the first of several mansions in what was to became a very exclusive Hollywood Hills neighborhood. Sid Grauman, owner of the famed Chinese Theater, L. Frank Baum, author of *The Wizard of Oz*, and producer Sam Goldwyn lived nearby. The Lane family occupied the mansion from the time it was constructed until the early 1940s. The house then went through several incarnations, including being used as a duplex style, multifamily home, a home for the elderly, and in the 1950s, it was divided into even smaller apartments. By 1960, the building was in such bad shape, it was scheduled for demolition.

In 1962, Hollywood producer Milt Larsen spotted the building and had an idea for rebuilding the mansion and turning it into a private club for magicians. The renovation took nearly a year to complete, and on January 2, 1963, the world-famous mansion opened its doors as home to the Academy of Magical Arts, Inc.

Over the next few years, Larsen continued his renovation, expanding the building and creating new wings. To this day, old rooms are occasionally refurbished, new special effects and artifacts are added, and the castle continues to grow and improve.

There are so many ancient artifacts and fixtures both inside and outside the house, it's no wonder that the mansion has the reputation for being haunted. The ornate three globe lamps in front of the house, for example, were originally street lights in Philadelphia, circa 1900. A fountain across from the entrance is constructed from a number of fountain pieces that once graced several mansions. The colorful background in the Grand Salon bar is a mosaic of theater lantern slides from the Hippodrome Theater in Los Angeles that were used to advertise coming attractions and performers scheduled to appear at the famous vaudeville theater. Each and every room in the castle is made up of relics from the past.

I was lucky enough to visit the mansion some time ago and I can vouch for the fact that walking through the Magic Castle's hand-carved front doors is like stepping back in time. The Victorian era is reflected in the rich woodwork, ceiling paintings, and furnishings that fill each room of the house. To set the mystical theme, guests immediately notice that this room has no doors, and in order to actually get further inside, visitors are asked to walk up to a small gilded owl with blinking eyes who is perched on a nearby bookcase. He serves as the guardian of the mansion, and the only way he will let you in is if you whisper the phrase "Open Sesame." The bookcase will then reveal a secret passage that leads inside.

While the mansion boasts several lively spirits in residence, The Hat and Hare Pub in the Haunted Wine Cellar, The Houdini Room, where each evening, twelve guests gather to participate in a séance, and Irma's Room seem to be some of the most lively areas.

After climbing down a narrow staircase into the hallway leading to the pub, which is actually constructed of parts of a number of antique British pubs and saloons, the first thing one sees is a large chandelier from MGM studios, which decorated dozens of movie sets in the 30s and 40s. The walls of the pub are covered with a myriad of authentic pub signs and advertisements from Great Britain, and the room gives off the feeling of a classic horror film setting complete with stone walls, warped wood, and little surprises hidden away in the walls and cabinetry.

One can't help but wonder whether the spirits of MGM's brightest stars ever drop in for an ethereal nightcap, and if they do, are they served by a ghostly British bartender from long ago?

When you step through the secret passageway that leads to The Houdini Room, you are actually entering one of the turrets that dominate the exterior of the house. Displayed throughout the room are priceless personal artifacts of Harry Houdini, the man who is generally accepted by the public as the "Greatest Magician in History." Amid an interesting collection of Houdiniania, including various pieces from séances in which Houdini either attended or conducted, and a large collection of handcuffs the magician used in performing his escape challenges, nightly visitors join hands to see if they can call upon the great Houdini himself.

Prior to his death on Halloween night in 1926, the famed illusionist made a pact with his wife Bessie that if was possible for his spirit to break through the barrier and return to the living, he would contact her. Mrs. Houdini tried for a decade to contact her dearly departed husband with questionable results. On January 9, 1929, she signed an affidavit confirming that his spirit had come through and communicated in a code that the two had devised prior to Houdini's death. Soon after that, and for the rest of her life, Bessie waffled, not in the conviction that the correct message came through, but whether or not it was her husband who had sent it.

Whether or not the nightly séance has ever actually made contact with the great Houdini, or any other of the castle's sprightly spirits is anybody's guess, but it's more than likely that at one time or another, visitors to the Magic Castle have encountered a spirit or two, even if they weren't aware of it. After all, apparitions sometimes appear to be quite solid and very much alive.

As for the Castle's other ghosts, there are reports that the ghost of a magician who died on stage is still seen in the theater where he last performed. There is also a reported encounter that took place in one of the ladies' rooms between a guest and a female spirit. And then there's Irma.

According to legend, Irma was one of the seven sisters who originally inhabited the house at the turn of the century. None of the other family members were musically inclined, but Irma was and she subscribed to a mail-order piano course. Her endless practicing was so irritating to the rest of the family that she and her piano were relegated to a small room in the tower. Irma became so embittered with the banishment that when she died, she vowed to return to haunt the house.

When the Sohmar grand piano was moved back to the Music Chamber many years later, it seemed that Irma's ghost returned with it, and most nights she takes her place at the piano and plays for the guests of the castle. The bartender often places a glass of spirits with a straw near the keyboard and it is soon drained. Irma plays a little less surely after that, but she always tries to answer requests, except for songs written after 1932, because that's the year that she died.

Skeptics claim that the music is played by a hidden, live pianist on a keyboard that is mechanically mated to Irma's keyboard and that the drinks are emptied through a hole in the bottom of the glass. While the management doesn't like to play up the ghostly aspect of the house and even refused to let us come out and investigate, they are said to sneer at such ridiculous un-occult thoughts about Irma.

The Hollywood Wax Museum

6767 Hollywood Boulevard, Hollywood, California 90028

When the Hollywood Wax Museum opened in 1966, people lined up for blocks to rub elbows with the likenesses of their favorite stars. They claimed that the wax figures were so lifelike, they wanted to reach out and touch them.

People from all over the world still come to admire the animated sets and wax figures, but many visitors get a little more than they originally paid for because the Hollywood Wax Museum is full of ghosts, and rumor has it that these disembodied spirits move among the wax figures.

The museum building has been home to a variety of businesses over the years. During the 1930s, the second floor of the building, which is now the Stella Adler Academy, once hosted the Embassy Club, a private dining venue for celebrities which is said to have been Hollywood's first nightclub. Before the Wax Museum moved in, the building was home to a luggage company, and the museum's current Operations Manager, Marc Agena, was told that the luggage company might have been a front for organized crime. "And during the 1920s," said Marc, "the basement of the building was used as a speakeasy, so who's to say who might be buried beneath us that we're not aware of."

A sign posted at the museum's entrance warns visitors that the building is haunted. It explains that the location was once the site of a business that burned down, killing an employee who was sleeping on the job, and whose ghost now haunts the museum. While some might consider this warning to be "Hollywood hype," there have been reports of cold spots, lights going off and on all by themselves, and disembodied voices heard throughout the building. Is that sleeping employee continually reliving his tragic death, or do some of Hollywood's greatest stars pop in from time to time to admire their likenesses?

Another possible resident ghost could be that of Spoony Singh, founder of the Hollywood Wax Museum, who passed away in October 2006. It was his vision to create a museum "where people screamed instead of tiptoed." One of his favorite stunts was to place breathing actors among the wax figures so visitors would be startled by sudden movements. Fearing lawsuits, (and the reported heart attack of a woman visitor) the museum ended the practice of "live scares" more than a decade ago, but the museum's resident ghosts don't seem to be breaking any rules when they decide to scare someone, because after all, they aren't technically alive.

Two to three million people visit the Wax Museum each year, including a host of celebrities who come in to check out their likenesses, and many people have reported seeing and hearing things they weren't expecting, especially around closing time. Some even have tangible proof that the museum is indeed haunted.

"A woman from England was here not long ago," said Marc, "and when she got back home she called me and asked if we had any kind of strange activity going on in the museum because when she had her pictures developed, they came back with huge shiny orbs on several of the pictures she took. She was so concerned by the eerie images that she had her camera checked out by experts who concluded that nothing was wrong with her equipment and stated that the anomalies were within the photos. She *FedExed* the photos to me and I saw them for myself."

Tourists aren't the only ones who have experienced strange goings on. About a year ago, manager Joseph Pascua was closing up the museum at midnight when he had his own scary encounter.

We also photographed orbs at the Last Supper exhibit.

"There were only two of us working that night and the other guy was outside," said Joseph. "I was turning off the breakers near the door that leads to the Chamber of Horrors when all of a sudden, the door slammed shut, really hard, all by itself. I immediately broke out in goose bumps, the hair stood up on the back of my neck and all I could do was try to get away from there. There was no wind in the building and since I was all alone, it had to have been a ghost that slammed the door."

Marc Agena admits that he and other staff members hear disembodied footsteps and strange noises all the time, but he had his first real supernatural encounter at the museum shortly after he began working there four years ago.

"I came in one weekend morning very early, about 7:00 AM and was in the process of turning on the lights in the center of the museum when I saw a mist coming up from the floor. It looked like something created by a fog machine. I also felt moisture in the air and immediately thought that there was a problem in the facility, like a water leak or a seepage from underground so I went to look for the maintenance engineer. I was only gone for a minute or two and when I came back, there was nothing there. I did a thorough search but couldn't find anything, so I just let it go. Then about a year later I hired a new employee and one day we were sitting and talking, and he started telling me about having seen the same phenomenon."

Explorations in Wax

With such a stellar reputation for ghosts and hauntings, it seemed natural to go and explore the Wax Museum and find out for myself whether any of these ghostly rumors were true. Just in case they were, and since it was decided that the investigation would take place at midnight when the spirits were likely to be more active, I asked psychic and paranormal investigator Victoria Gross, investigator/cameraman Barry Conrad, and Hollywood historian Scott Michaels to come along.

We met Marc at the back door just before midnight, and after walking through a maze of dismembered body parts and severed heads in the storeroom, we made our way down one of the world's narrowest hallways into the employee lounge where we sat down and worked out a game plan for our investigation.

It was initially decided that I would walk around with Victoria to see where the hot spots of activity might be while Barry set up to film interviews with the employees who had had paranormal experiences in the museum. Then, armed with digital cameras and walkie-talkies to keep in touch, we walked downstairs into the museum. Barry, Scott, and the museum crew took off in different directions, but because Victoria immediately felt a strong male presence at the foot of the stairs, she and I stayed behind to see what she was picking up.

A curious orb is watching us set up.

"He's a big man, very tall with black hair and olive skin and he's not from this time," she said. "I'd say he goes back to the 1920s or 30s and I'm getting the name Joe or Joseph."

Just as she said that, Victoria felt as though someone hit her hard in the upper back and had to steady herself because she began feeling quite dizzy.

"I'm feeling a sharp pain in my back right now and I also feel a great deal of confusion," she explained. "I think something bad happened to him here on this spot. This isn't residual energy," she went on to say, "This is an active haunting even though Joseph keeps fading in and out. I don't feel as though he ever leaves this area, nor does the woman in a long black dress who I can see going up the steps. This whole area right here is very active."

Because Victoria's dizziness was not subsiding, we decided to leave Joseph and the woman for a while and join the others.

We met up with Barry and Scott at the entrance to the dark and foreboding Chamber of Horrors, and found out that Barry was also feeling dizzy and a bit disoriented. "It's the kind of dizziness that makes you feel like you're underneath several fathoms of water," he said, but after walking further into the chamber, the atmosphere quickly changed. Victoria felt the presence of a woman near the Hell Boy exhibit, and when Barry took a picture of the area with his digital camera in the dungeon, he caught a couple of bright orbs.

Scott and I decided to continue on through the Chamber leaving Barry and Victoria to continue their investigation.

I was kind of spooked as we walked along the dark corridor admiring the likenesses of Bela Lugosi, Boris Karloff and others of that ilk, and soon we were far enough away from the rest of the group that we didn't hear them talking anymore. When we stopped to admire the Betelgeuse display, both Scott and I suddenly heard the distinct sound of scurrying, shuffling footsteps nearby. There was clearly nobody else around, and since neither of us were brave enough to continue down the corridor by ourselves to chase down the phantom, we stayed rooted to the spot for a few minutes until Victoria and Barry caught up with us.

Orbs in the Chamber of Horrors dungeon.

After we told Victoria what we'd both just heard, she explained that she was picking up the spirit of a man, dressed in costume with a long dark cape and top hat, who continually walks the halls in a sort of pattern.

"This is a person who is drawn to the macabre," Victoria explained. "He's a bit of a demented soul, but I don't feel he would hurt anybody. The guy is really okay and pleased just to be here, and I think he's just someone who really feels comfortable in these surroundings. This was his world. What's interesting is that at first I picked him up as being old, but now I'm sensing him as a teenager. I wonder if he's showing me both," she mused.

As she was describing the male spirit who seemed to be dressed in costume with a long cape and top hat, we all heard what sounded like a loud moan, followed by a disturbing grumble. Could that have been his way of confirming her information?

Because we felt as though someone was trying to communicate with us, we invited any spirits that were there to make their presence known and talk to us, hoping that our request would result in some stunning EVPs (electronic voice phenomenon), but apparently those particular entities preferred to be seen but not heard and remained mum.

While most of the wax figures throughout the museum seemed rather "dead" and lifeless, Victoria did come across one or two that she felt actually contained a spirit. "There are some of these likenesses that you can just sense an energy within and that's because they do actually contain a human spirit," she explained. "Some earthbound spirits don't want to cross over, and these figures are the closest thing they have to a real body and they will settle for the next best thing. It's like when you go into bars, there are a lot of what we call "astral hitchhikers" because they are spirits who are drinking and smoking through the living people who are there."

One of the mannequins in which Victoria sensed a spirit presence was the Jude Law figurine on the Hollywood Boulevard set, and another is one of the crucified mannequins

Could this orb be the spirit of Charlie Chaplin?

in The Last Supper display which, according to Marc, is one of the most actively haunted areas in the entire museum.

Both Victoria and Scott felt extremely uncomfortable around The Last Supper, the oldest exhibit in the museum. "I feel really disturbed by this, even more so than the horror displays," she noted. "Something isn't right about this whole area. There's something kind of sinister here, and for some reason, I get the feeling that evil is attracted to this display."

Marc pointed out one of the wax figures sitting at the table who had a broken finger and said that this happens quite often despite the fact that the display is set back into its own niche and visitors have no access to it. To Marc and the others who work there, the mystery of the broken fingers is more puzzling than the DaVinci Code.

Just opposite the eerie display is a bench where Victoria saw the spirit of a very forlorn woman sitting and staring at the image of Christ. "She's very upset and is giving off a strong sense of longing. It's as though she's staring at the display and longing for what Christ represents."

Because both Victoria and Scott were feeling so uncomfortable in the area, we decided to move along but didn't get far before encountering yet another lost soul.

Another Last Supper exhibit orb.

Just as we approached the Spiderman display, Victoria commented that her third eye was really tingling, then she began having trouble breathing, and oddly enough, began walking in circles.

"I'm here on the street, I'm lost and I'm so scared," she kept repeating over and over again. "I just want to cry."

When I pressed her for details about whose energy she was sensing, she explained that this was a young blond girl, about eighteen years old, whose name was Sarah. "She's not from here," said Victoria. "She came to Hollywood, probably as a runaway and ended up being murdered around this area twenty or thirty years ago.

"Lots of spirits come in here off the boulevard," she went on to explain. "Hollywood is a transient place, so you're going to have transient ghosts. I don't think that a lot of the spirits around here are crossed over, nor do they want to be."

While Victoria doesn't believe in helping to cross spirits over that seem to be happy here on the earth plane, she feels that sometimes it is necessary to help those who are in distress as Sarah obviously was. After calling out for assistance from a higher being to help Sarah move on, Victoria sensed a very loving energy come in, possibly Sarah's mother or grand-mother, who had come to take the young girl's troubled spirit to a better place. As soon as the energy entered the room, Victoria felt Sarah calm down quite a bit and got the feeling that she knew the woman spirit who had come rescue her. The two entities began to communicate with each other and then Sarah willingly went with her towards the light. When we came back to the area later that night, Sarah had indeed gone.

The submarine corridor for the *Hunt For Red October* ex-hibit was another spot that felt quite disturbing. It's an area that you need to walk through to get back to the front of the museum. Because the museum was in semi-darkness at that point, it was a particularly foreboding area to walk through, and sensing a presence lurking about that wasn't particularly friendly, Victoria drew a banishing pentagram in the air for protection before we even entered the area. Then, as we quickly walked through, she explained that standing next to the walls on either side of us were spirits watching us go by. I secretly hoped that none of them would be tempted to reach out and touch one of us — and thankfully they didn't. But a few minutes later, as we were standing in front of the *Wizard of Oz* display, something definitely brushed past my hand. And later on in the evening while admiring the likenesses of Michael Landon, Lorne Greene, and Dan Blocker at the *Bonanza* display, it felt as though someone was tickling my elbow. Victoria said that something touched her left arm as we were standing there as well.

She also picked up the spirit of a large, dignified man in his 60s, who was standing nearby. He appeared to be leaning over the railing and was looking appreciatively at the display. "This man is from the 1940s, and while the museum wasn't here then, this man was, and," she added, "he still is. He's one of those spirits who enjoy walking up and down Hollywood Boulevard. He goes in and out of the various restaurants and businesses along the way. I see him as a dignified man who was probably associated with the motion picture industry. He knows he's dead, so he may have already crossed over and just comes back once in a while to keep an eye on things."

Because there are so many spirits hanging around throughout the building, Victoria suggested that we return at a later date and conduct a séance to get a little more up close and personal with the ghosts of the Hollywood Wax Museum. And next time you're in Hollywood, you may want to do a little ghost hunting at the museum on your own, so don't forget to bring your camera because Wax Museum ghosts are not the least bit camera shy.

Hollywood Center Studios

1040 N. Las Palmas Avenue
Hollywood, California 90038

Hollywood Center Studios has been around since 1914, when designer John Jasper, a veteran of Charlie Chaplin's filmmaking mill for thirteen years, quit Chaplin Studios to build three production stages on a stretch of undeveloped Hollywood property and dubbed it Hollywood Studios, Inc. Harold Lloyd made silent films there in the 20s, and when silent films turned into "talkies," Howard Hughes came to the lot to film *Hell's Angels*. In 1930, Hughes left for new digs a few blocks away at United Artists, and in 1935, after scandalizing the Hays Office with *Belle of the Nineties*, Mae West arrived on the lot with strict orders from Paramount to clean up her act.

In the early 1940s, Douglas Fairbanks, Jr., Stan Laurel and Oliver Hardy, Fred Astaire, Cary Grant, and Erich von Stroheim were all at the studio making movies. Then in 1945, William Cagney, brother and partner of actor James Cagney, purchased a substantial interest in the studio and moved his offices there.

Comedy legends Burns and Allen arrived during the early fifties, and cigar smoking George kept an office on the lot until his death at the age of 100 in 1996. Sadly, the building that housed Burns' office was victim to a fire several years ago, and no longer exists.

In 1951, Ronald Reagan shot *The Last Outpost* at the studio and Lucille Ball and Desi Arnaz rented Stage 2 to shoot *I Love Lucy*. They retrofitted the stage for the series and stayed on the lot for two years. During that time, Lucy and Desi formed their own company, Desilu, and the show was moved over to the former RKO Pictures lot which Desilu had purchased. Stage 2 is also rumored to be the place where Shirley Temple made her film debut in either the "Baby Burlesk" short, *War Babies* or *What To Do?* depending on which source you believe.

By 1952, CBS was renting out space and had thirteen shows in production on the lot which by then had changed it's name to General Service Studios. From that point on, the studio continued to service a full load of television productions including *Ozzie and Harriet, Mr. Ed, Green Acres, The Beverly Hillbillies, The Lone Ranger,* and *The Addams Family.*

A new rock and roll client base, including Stevie Wonder, Lionel Richie, Crosby, Stills & Nash, Michael Jackson, and Ray Charles began shooting music videos and specials there starting in the 1960s, director Francis Ford Coppola bought the studio in 1980, and after that, independent feature film producers, as well as the music industry, often used the lot to make movies, such as *Body Heat* and *When Harry Met Sally.*

These days, Hollywood Center Studios is still doing a lively business, but while productions may come and go, it's been said that some of the famous people who used to call the lot their "home away from home" haven't gone anywhere.

When psychic Chris Fleming was there for the taping of an episode on Lucille Ball for his television show, *Dead Famous: Ghostly Encounters*, the spirits of both Lucille Ball and Desi Arnaz made an appearance on their old sound stage, but Chris feels that the main haunting on Stage 2 was caused by someone who, strangely enough, had no ties to show business at all. "It was the spirit of a small boy, about nine years old," said Chris, "and he wanted to be heard."

Chris says that the young boy's ghost dates back to the early 1900s when the studio first opened for business, a fact he garnered by the little boy's attire of knickers and a "news-boy cap" of that era. Chris surmises that this boy's father probably worked at the studio or had some attachment to it and it was a big thing for the dad to show his son how motion pictures were made. "That's why the boy kind of hung around all those years, because the place made him feel so good. And when we were there, he was excited that he was actually recognized and finally had the opportunity to communicate with someone."

"About six to eight months after we filmed that investigation at the studio, the little boy came through to me again," said Chris. "I was with a friend of mine, Tom, who was doing some channeling, and all of a sudden I felt the need to channel as well. I felt this little boy's spirit coming through, and I was blown away by that because, at the time, I thought that a spirit that was here on the earth plane had to remain at a specific location. And here was this boy who had been on the earth plane for many years, and was mad and upset that no one ever talked to him, and come to find out that the boy had actually been following me around all that time because I was the only one who had actually spoken to him. It was a learning experience for me to have something like that happen.

"What we actually did at that time was to cross him over," said Chris. "Tom first asked if he wanted us to help him, and it was interesting because Tom was assisting as the boy was speaking through me. Then all of a sudden the boy said 'Jesus! Jesus appeared!' and then he was gone. I was seeing the image that the boy saw through his eyes, and there was Jesus with open arms and the boy just took off right to him. Just being a bystander and seeing something like that meant something to me. It was confirmation for me as well as for the other people who assisted in this crossing over. It was pretty amazing, and a great ending chapter to the story."

That wasn't the last time that a spirit decided to follow Chris home, however. Not long ago, he was doing an investigation at the famous, and very haunted Stanley Hotel in Colorado with the TAPS crew from the television series *Ghost Hunters*. The hotel was Stephen King's inspiration for writing his best selling novel, *The Shining*, because he claims to have had several paranormal experiences while staying there.

When Chris got back home after the investigation, he started feeling as though his energy was being drained; he said that he'd get up in the morning and hear someone calling his name right beside the bed and his doors were opening and closing on their own. "My cat freaked out, got up on the bed and was looking right at this thing, howling, and I think part of it was that the entity was manipulating the cat and making it do that," he recalls. "It took me about a week and a half to get rid of it and I had to call someone to come in and help me out. I hated what was going on because in addition to the experience being physically draining, it put me into a depressive state and gave me thoughts that were not my own. You've really got to be careful going out on investigations like that. Society doesn't understand how much harm some entities can actually do. More than we can ever imagine."

The Knickerbocker Hotel

1714 N. Ivar Avenue, Hollywood, California 90028

The Knickerbocker Hotel is a historic Los Angeles Hotel, and over the years, it has had more than its share of notoriety. Now a senior citizen's home called the Hollywood Knickerbocker Apartments, in its heyday, the hotel was the scene for some of Hollywood's most famous dramatic moments, which, in the grand Hollywood tradition includes suicides, séances, and quite a few deaths.

Built in 1925, the hotel played a key role throughout the boisterous 1920s. It first opened its doors as a luxury apartment building, then in later years transformed itself into a hotel. One of the hotel's main attractions was the Renaissance Revival bar which played host to the Hollywood elite. One frequent guest was silent screen star Rudolph Valentino, who, as legend has it, would ride his horse down from the Ivar Hills to drink and dance the tango to live music in the hotel's posh Lido Room which hosted many parties for Hollywood stars.

At one time or another, Mae West, Barbara Stanwyck, Lana Turner, Frank Sinatra, Larry Fine of The Three Stooges, Laurel and Hardy, Cecil B. DeMille, and many others have all lived at the Knickerbocker Hotel. Marilyn Monroe spent her honeymoon with Joe Dimaggio there and Elvis Presley stayed in suite 1016 in 1956 while he was shooting *Love Me Tender*. He also posed for *Heartbreak Hotel* publicity photos in one of the rooms. Fellow rocker Jerry Lee Lewis also used to stay at the hotel whenever he was in town.

The hotel lobby features a huge crystal chandelier, which cost over $120,000 in 1925, and it was under this chandelier that epic film director D. W. Griffith died of a stroke in 1948. At the time of his death, Griffith, who was a pioneer in the Hollywood film industry, had been largely forgotten by his peers. He eeked out a painful and lonely existence at the Knickerbocker spending most of his time in the hotel bar talking to anyone who would listen to him. His dismissal by Hollywood was as great a tragedy and it would not be until years later that he would be regarded as the genius that he undoubtedly was.

The first instance of a supernatural nature to occur at the Knickerbocker was the anniversary séance to contact the spirit of magician Harry Houdini. For ten years after his death, Houdini's wife Bess held séances in the hopes of communicating with her late husband. The last "official" Houdini séance was held on Halloween night in 1936. A group of friends, fellow magicians, and Bess herself gathered on the roof of the Knickerbocker Hotel and attempted to contact the elusive magician for over an hour before finally giving up. At the moment they all got up to leave, a tremendously violent thunderstorm broke out, drenching the séance participants and terrifying them with the horrific lightning and thunder. They would later find out that this mysterious storm did not occur anywhere else in Hollywood...only above the Knicker-bocker Hotel.

Actor William Frawley, who played crusty Fred Mertz on the *I Love Lucy* show, lived at the hotel for decades until March of 1966 when he was walking into the Knickerbocker and dropped dead of a heart attack on the sidewalk just outside the door.

The hotel is prominently featured in the tragic life of ac-tress Frances Farmer, a huge name in Hollywood in the 1930s and 1940s. By the age of twenty-seven she had made eighteen films, starred in three Broadway plays, and appeared in thirty-two major radio shows. But at the pinnacle of her professional career, Frances began having problems in her personal life. She began to drink and take drugs for weight control which caused her to act erratically on the set, and she soon became a problem to those she worked with. In 1943, she got into a fight at the Knickerbocker and the police dragged her, half naked, through the lobby and off to jail.

At her hearing the next morning, all accounts agree that the actress behaved quite erratically. She claimed the police had violated her civil rights, demanded an attorney, and proceeded to throw an inkwell at the judge, who immediately sentenced her to 180 days in jail. When the judge asked if she had had anything to drink since the last time she was in court, she replied that she'd drunk anything she came upon and also that she had been taking Benzedrine. She then knocked down a policeman and ran to a nearby phone booth where she tried to call her attorney. She was subdued by the police who physically carried her away as she shouted, "Have you ever had a broken heart?"

Farmer was then transferred to the psychiatric ward of Los Angeles General Hospital and diagnosed with "manic depressive psychosis." Within days she was transferred to the San Fernando Valley and the Kimball Sanitarium in La Crescenta. There, Farmer was diagnosed with paranoid schizophrenia and received insulin shock therapy, which her family later said was given without their consent. These tortuous treatments went on for seven years. During that time Farmer managed to escape once but was caught.

According to some sources, the actress was eventually given a lobotomy and released as cured, but whether or not she actually was lobotomized is questionable. The one certainty is that after all the various treatments she actually was subjected to, she was no longer the same person. The hospital stay and treatment had destroyed the actress. She died alone and broke of esophageal cancer at the ages of fifty-seven. Many people claim to have seen the ghost of Frances Farmer walking the halls of the Knickerbocker and it's their feeling that the actress will never be able to rest.

Perhaps the hotel's strangest tragedy took place in November 1962 with the suicide of Irene Gibbons, a costume designer at MGM. Gibbons designed outfits for a number of famous actresses including Marlene Dietrich, Elizabeth Taylor, Judy Garland, and Lana Turner. In 1962, after her friend, Doris Day, noticed that Irene seemed upset and nervous, Gibbons confided in her that she was in love with actor Gary Cooper and that he was the only man that she had ever loved. Unfortunately, Cooper had died of lung cancer the year before. Conflicting reports claim that Gibbons was actually upset over the medical condition of her husband who was paralyzed as the result of several strokes.

On the 15th of November at 2 AM, Irene checked into room 1129 at the Knickerbocker under an assumed name. During the next couple of hours she wrote a two page suicide note mentioning her husband's illness, and apologized to hotel guests for any inconvenience her death may cause. While plotting her demise, Irene polished off nearly two pints of Smirnoff. (Investigators later found two pint bottles, one empty and one with two shots left in it.) At 3:12 that afternoon, Gibbons pushed out the screen of her window and jumped to her death.

A Mr. Lombardo, who was staying in room 429 heard the crash on the roof and contacted the hotel manager, Mr. Tozzi, who discovered Irene on the third floor roof, nine feet in front of room 329. In her purse, which was left in the room along with the suicide note, there was $1.62 in cash, various cosmetics, three credit cards, and a drivers license. She was sixty years old.

The most haunted spot in the hotel was always thought to be the hotel bar, so when the Knickerbocker closed in 1971 and became a senior citizen's retirement building, the old bar was sealed off. The rooms remained unused for nearly twenty-five years until the early 1990s, when it was reopened as a nostalgic coffee shop called The All-Star Theater Café & Speakeasy. The art-deco cafe' hosted studio wrap parties and film shoots attracting the like of Sandra Bullock and Leonardo DiCaprio. In the film, *The Graduate*, the All Star Café bar is where Dustin Hoffman's character would meet Mrs. Robinson (Anne Bancroft). The chandeliers in the center of the All Star Café were said to have come from the kitchen of Liberace's Hollywood mansion as did an ice machine that Liberace kept in his own bar.

In addition to the very much alive celebrities who frequented the café, there have been a number of sprit sightings as well, particularly in the Ladies Vanity Room where cold spots were felt and light flashes appeared out of nowhere. There were also a few reported sightings of a little girl and boy running around the café and suddenly disappearing. The ghost of Marilyn Monroe was also reportedly seen in the women's restroom, and other anonymous spirits sometimes appeared to staff members.

The Avalon (Palace) Theater

1735 N. Vine Street, Hollywood, California 90028

This historic three-story building near the famous intersection of Hollywood and Vine was built in 1927 and was originally known as The Hollywood Playhouse. It was the first and most lavish legitimate theater in Hollywood at the time. Over the past eighty years, it has had many incarnations, including The WPA Federal Theater, El Capitan Theater, The Jerry Lewis Theater, The Hollywood Palace, and The Palace.

One of the four professional theaters in Hollywood, the venue has provided a showcase for many stars. Fanny Brice's radio program, *The Baby Snooks Radio Show*, and Ken Murray's popular *Blackouts Theater Revue*, (1942-1949) made their homes here. As the times changed, the theater became one of television's first studios. *This is Your Life, The Hollywood Palace, The Lawrence Welk Show*, and many Bob Hope specials were filmed there. In 1964, The Beatles had their first West Coast performance in the building prior to their legendary appearance at the Hollywood Bowl, and over the years, each ex-Beatle would also take the stage as a solo artist. President Richard Nixon gave his Checkers speech in 1952 from the stage on a set that was built to resemble his living room, and President Bill Clinton gave his historic "Gays In The Military" speech from The Palace in 1992.

Carmen Miranda, "The Brazilian Bombshell," gave her last performance at the theater on August 4, 1955 in the *Colgate Comedy Hour* hosted by Jimmy Durante. An A&E Network *Biography* episode featuring Carmen Miranda contained the tragic kinescope footage from that appearance. After completing her dance number, Miranda unknowingly suffered a mild heart attack, and nearly collapsed onstage. Durante ran to her side and helped to keep the stricken actress on her feet. Carmen then regained her composure, smiled, and waved to the audience; then walked offstage for the last time. The lady with the tutti-frutti hat was gone by the next morning. She was just forty-six years old.

In 1963, the building was turned into The Jerry Lewis Theatre and was home to the comedian's weekly ABC-TV variety series. When the program failed, ABC raised a more classic title onto the marquee, The Hollywood Palace, and launched its hit *Hollywood Palace* series with a kaleidoscope of show business greats from Judy Garland to Louis Armstrong.

After that show was canceled in 1970, the theater kept on going as the ABC studio where a number of variety shows were produced. Merv Griffin used the facility for his popular talk show before moving to a place all his own just down the street, while Chuck Barris used the venue to tape *The Dating Game* and *The Newlywed Game* on weekends.

The Hollywood Palace then took a well-deserved breather until a local businessman purchased the property in 1978. After four years of careful planning, painstaking restoration, and massive refurbishing, the theater opened once again as The Palace, which became the hottest concert venue and nightclub in town. Prince, Madonna, The Rolling Stones, and others of that ilk regularly came to party at The Palace. Olivia Newton John even had her wedding reception there. It's said that some bands, like The Rolling Stones, performed there just because it was The Palace.

Hundreds of legendary performers have left their imprints on the famous stage over the years so it's no wonder that the building is now considered haunted. Strangely enough though, none of the resident ghosts seem to be celebrities, but they have been sighted so often, they are famous in their own right.

It's reported that the many ghosts at The Avalon seem to be most active in the early morning hours, their favorite time being around 2:30 AM.

"Emily" is said to be a former chorus girl who worked at the theater. Her apparition has not been seen but can frequently be *heard* waking across the south side second floor hallway in high heels. Another entity called "Harry" has been identified as a former theater electrician and has been encountered throughout the building. Generally mischievous in nature, Harry likes to tie ropes and cables in knots and steal tools. He might also be the one responsible for the stage lighting that seems to turn on and off by itself, as well as other electrical anomalies that often plague the theater. Harry's name can be seen on the walls of the fly gallery. Legend has it that an electrician did actually die backstage during one of the shows.

Many patrons in the main lobby women's lounge have reported a girl crying in one of the stalls, while others report hearing voices in the balcony, around the main bars, and on the main floor. A glowing blue light has been seen moving about the main room of the theater by several employees and there are a couple of known "cold spots" as well. One is at the backstage stairs on the south side of the building and the other is the first row of the balcony where many have seen shadowy figures.

Another spirit has been know to slide paperwork out from under the accounting office door when there is definitely no one inside. Could a former employee still be hard at work in the afterlife?

The only "negative energy" ghost in the building is described as a tall featureless shadowy figure of a man in a hat. He's been seen in the basement hallway and is also attributed to the creepy stay-away feelings that are sometimes felt near the north basement stairs and the south production area.

One workman reported that while he was working alone in a remote location inside the ceiling, he was startled by a voice directly behind him that called out, "Hey... hey you!"

In the '90's, before The Palace installed its sophisticated security system, they had a large, burly night guard who also reported some eerie experiences.

Early one morning while making his rounds, the guard heard some beautiful piano music coming from the third floor comedy room. Wanting to find out who was in there that shouldn't be, he went to investigate. The door was locked, but a strange light was emanating from the room. He carefully slipped the key into the door and opened it, but when he did, the music suddenly stopped and the light disappeared. The piano was uncovered and the bench pulled out, but no one was there.

Another night after closing, the guard was locking up the second floor lobby and had a strange sensation he later described as an unseen presence. A cold wind gently blew past him and he could smell the scent of a sweet perfume. As he headed for the stairs, someone tapped him gently on the shoulder but when he turned around, there was no one there.

Eventually, this guard became quite leery of being at the theater all alone, so he brought his cousin's German Shepherd to work with him for moral support. One night as he was sitting at one of the tables in the main room on the first floor reading the paper, the dog suddenly looked intently at the left side of the stage. Both man and dog went over to investigate and were shocked to see the transparent figure of a man wearing a tuxedo looking back at them. The dog took off after the apparition but it quickly disappeared.

After that incident, the guard decided to set a trap in the kitchen area by putting a plate on the floor with a wine glass on top of it, thinking that if something went through the kitchen, it probably wouldn't see this obstacle and knock it over. A short while later he heard a noise coming from the kitchen and the dog bounded in after it but quickly came back, whining like a puppy and obviously quite frightened. When the guard then went to investigate, he found that while nobody was there the plate had been placed on top of the wine glass.

Another night, while standing alone on the main dance floor, a guard looked up to the balcony where he saw an older couple talking together. After calling up to them to say that they couldn't be up there, he got no response, so he charged up the stairs to the balcony to confront them face to face. As he approached the couple, he saw that they were dressed in 1930s theater attire, and within the blink of an eye, they were gone. Patrons of the theater often complain about a noisy couple talking and laughing in the balcony in this same spot where the apparitions have been seen.

A theater operations manager in the '90s also had some strange experiences. One night after closing, all the lights had been shut off, but when he came back into the club a few minutes later, all the stage lights had been turned back on. Then suddenly the lights turned themselves off again and the stage was just dimly lit by the blue lights on the cat walk above the stage. Just then, a shimmering wavy five-foot square mass floated across the stage and back before it completely disappeared.

According to Joel Huxtable, the theater's lighting designer, it seems as though three of Avalon's ghosts (which he feels were most probably residual hauntings to begin with) have left the building. "Hank and Mary, the older, well-dressed couple, are no longer seen — I believe — because the opera box they were seen in was demolished for renovation, and a new opera box was constructed. This also seems to be true for my personal favorite, Emily, who walked the halls upstairs. She has also not been heard since demolition/construction of the offices upstairs."

Even if some of the theater's ghosts may have gone, no doubt many others are still in the wings waiting for their time in the limelight.

Silent Movie Theatre

611 N Fairfax Ave, Los Angeles, California 90036

When I was growing up, it was always a treat when my parents took me to the Silent Movie Theatre. Watching the black and white films with subtitles and accompanied by live organ music was great fun, but we didn't go very often because my mother said the hard wooden seats literally gave her a pain in the— well, you know.

The theater was opened by Mr. John Hampton in 1942, fifteen years after silent films had become passé, and the films he ran were from his personal collection. Most of the patrons during the 1940s came to the theater to rewatch the movies of their childhood, and a number of old-time actors used to drop by to watch their old films.

In 1981, Hampton was forced to close the theater due to illness and financial problems, and it stayed closed until Hampton's death in 1990. It was then purchased by Laurence Austin and reopened in 1991.

Over the years, the theater has garnered a reputation not only as a venue for nostalgia, but also for its two resident ghosts. It is known to be haunted by the spirits of two former owners. John Hampton regularly haunts the upstairs lounge which used to be his and his wife Dorothy's apartment for over forty-five years, and the second ghost is that of Laurence Austin, whose spirit is regularly seen in the lobby. Austin was shot and killed during an apparent robbery attempt on January 17, 1997.

Around 8:30 that evening, a patron clad in black got up from his seat, went into the lobby, and pulled out a gun. Austin was in the tiny box office, counting money with a nineteen-year-old girl who worked for him. Confronted with a demand for the cash, they handed it over, and then for reasons that were not immediately apparent, the gunman opened fire. Laurence Austin was shot in the face at point-blank range and died instantly. The employee was shot in the chest.

The movie-goers first thought they were hearing fireworks until the robber ran down the aisle, firing more shots as he headed out a rear door of the tiny theater. Audience members dove under the seats as he fled into a back alley. Police later arrested Austin's partner, James Van Sickle, for hiring the gunman to kill Austin so that he could gain the inheritance. Both he and the gunman were arrested and are now serving life sentences for their crime.

In March of the following year, the theater was put up for sale and many people assumed that this would be the end of it, but the story had a happy ending when silent film enthusiast Charlie Lustman purchased the theater on impulse (he suspects that the spirit of John Hampton was spurring him on) and then reopened it in November of 1999 as the only silent film cinema in the USA. In June 2006, brothers Dan and Sammy Harkham bought the theater, and while they are still running silent films, they are planning to mix in sound programming as well.

This a very small theater, with only 224 seats, but there is still live music (organ or piano) accompanying the movies starring the likes of Laurel and Hardy, Mary Pickford, and The Keystone Cops. Before the main feature begins, you can expect to see silent shorts, cartoons, and serials, but if you happen to venture into the lobby for a quick snack, don't be alarmed if the hair on the back of your neck stands up or you feel as though you're being watched. It's probably just one of the former owners making sure that you're having a good time.

Greystone Mansion

905 Loma Vista Drive, Beverly Hills, California 90210

In the late 1920s, the Greystone Mansion was home to Edward Doheny, Jr., his wife, Lucy, and their five children. In 1910, Doheny's father, the fabulously wealthy oilman, Edward L. Doheny Sr., bought 429 acres in the Beverly Hills area after striking it rich in the 1890s. He gave a 12.58-acre plot to his son Edward (Ned) as a wedding present in 1914, but the younger Doheny and his wife left the land alone until 1925. The Gothic English-style house, the largest private estate in Los Angeles, took three years to build at a cost of $3.1 million dollars. The family moved into the newly completed house, which included 55 livable rooms (67 in all) including stable apartments in 46,054 square feet in September 1928.

On the night of February 16, 1929, only six months after the family moved in, Hugh Plunkett, a family chauffeur who eventually became Ned's personal secretary, arrived at the Greystone mansion. He called the house from the gates and was told by Lucy Doheny that he could not come in. Ignoring the request for him to leave, Hugh apparently used his pass key to enter the grounds and the house and went directly to the guest bedroom on the first floor where he often stayed.

Ned Doheny found him there around 10 PM. At 10:30, the Doheny family physician, E.C. Fishbaugh, who was in Hollywood attending a theater performance, received a frantic call from his maid who told him that he was needed urgently at the Doheny home. Fishbaugh arrived a little before 11 PM, and was greeted by Lucy Doheny who told him that Plunkett and her husband were in the guest bedroom. As they proceeded down the hallway, they noticed that the bedroom door was ajar and Plunkett was standing next to it. He warned them to come no closer, then shut the door and a shot rang out.

When the doctor barged into the room, he found Plunkett lying on the floor by the door shot through the head, the gun lying by his side. Doheny lay on the floor by the beds next to an overturned chair, barely alive, also with a gunshot wound to the head. He died soon after.

In the months prior to February 1929, Plunkett had divorced his wife and had been exhibiting signs of a nervous disorder. He had been taking medication, and there was talk among his doctor and the Dohenys of sending him to a sanatorium.

Investigators determined that Plunkett had taken a .45 caliber revolver from the Doheny garage and had shot Doheny, then turned the gun on himself. Testimony about Plunkett's unstable behavior over the previous six months, and Dr. Fishbaugh's testimony about the family's concern for Plunkett's sanity reinforced this finding and no formal inquest was held.

Over the years, questions have arisen about the events of that February night. Various rumors surfaced: that Plunkett and Doheny were more than just good friends, and that Lucy might have killed them in a fit of jealousy; or that Plunkett shot Doheny in a quarrel over his salary. Questions were raised about the timing of the killings. Was there a delay between the time of the deaths and the arrival of the police? Were the bodies moved to better suit the story told to the police? Was there an effort made to make Plunkett look crazy, to make the murder/suicide story more plausible? The undeniable wealth and influence of the Dohenys added to the public's fascination with the tragedy.

After Ned's death, Greystone was sold to Henry Crown of the Park Grey Corporation in Chicago for $1.5 million. Crown never occupied the building and the mansion was subsequently deeded to the City of Beverly Hills. In 1971, the City dedicated Greystone as a city park. In 1976, it was added to the Department of Interior's National Register of Historic Places.

There have been many ghost sightings on the property and the creepy stories about Greystone are quite famous. Stories of mysterious clouds of perfume, strange noises, lost objects original to the house being discovered in plain sight, pools of blood that mysteriously appear, then disappear, and many more. Film crews who use the mansion for location shoots also report strange happenings there. The mansion has been used for such films as *Spider-Man 3. The Witches of Eastwick*, in the TV miniseries *Winds of War, War and Remembrance*, and *Murder She Wrote*. Appropriately enough, the 1984 movie *Ghostbusters* also used Greystone as one of their shooting locations.

Several years ago, I visited Greystone with psychic Kenny Kingston and his associate, Valerie Porter. While the mansion itself was closed to the public, we were able to snoop around the outside and peer into the windows. Kenny sensed a great deal of sadness associated with the room where Ned Doheny was murdered, and in truth, the whole building had a rather spooky feel. While I didn't see any ghosts lurking about, I did see three bright orbs whiz past one of the windows in an otherwise dark room. Perhaps someone or something inside the mansion just wanted to get our attention and say hello.

CBS Columbia Square

6121 Sunset Boulevard, Hollywood, California 90028

The ghost of actor Bob Crane has been spotted by various witnesses at the old CBS Columbia studios along with the spirit of chief executive of CBS, William S. Paley, who passed away in 1990. Since Paley was responsible for building CBS from a small radio network to one of the most recognized television stations in the U. S., there is no wonder that his ghost has been seen from time to time.

Columbia Square was built in 1938 as a CBS radio studio, and was considered the most technologically advanced facility of its type at the time. It became home to some of the best-known comedies of radio's golden age. Jack Benny, Burns and Allen, Red Skelton, Eve Arden, Jack Oakie, and Steve Allen all broadcast their shows from the studio and the Columbia network broadcast big band music from nearby ballrooms including the nearby Hollywood Palladium and the Earl Caroll Theater.

The studio was built for KNX as the Columbia Broadcasting System's West Coast operations headquarters on the site of the Nestor Film Company, Hollywood's first movie studio. The Christie Film Company eventually took over operation and filmed comedies on the site, which was originally the location of an early Hollywood roadhouse.

The network began as a five-watt radio station operating from the Hollywood bedroom of Fred Christian, a former

Marconi wireless operator and radio salesman who wanted to provide broadcast content for customers who purchased his wireless sets. He played records borrowed from stores and became LA's first deejay. The station was then briefly owned by the *Los Angeles Evening Express*. Its signal was boosted to 50,000 watts in 1934 and was purchased by CBS founder William S. Paley in 1936, at a cost of $1.25 million, to expand his fledgling network's California presence and to tap into Hollywood's talent pool. Paley was anxious to feed the growing nationwide hunger for Hollywood movie stars on radio. The stars came, and following them were receptive audiences who lined up at all hours to watch the exciting live broadcasts performed by their favorite stars.

The Square's original configuration included eight studios. Studio B held 400 seats. Nearby, the Square's large auditorium was capable of seating 1,050 audience members. The entire complex included Brittingham's Radio Center Restaurant and a branch of the Bank of America. Tours of the studios cost forty cents. The facility produced both network and local programs and Columbia Square became a magnet for Hollywood's top stars, writers, musicians, and producers. While the network news and soap operas continued to originate in New York, the CBS/KNX facility produced the bulk of Columbia's classic old-time radio dramas and comedies. James Dean worked for a brief time as an usher at Columbia Square and the pilot for *I Love Lucy* was filmed on the Square's stages in TV's early years.

In later years, some of the Square's once-luxurious radio theaters were converted to recording studios for Columbia Records where Bob Dylan and Barbra Streisand, among many top stars, recorded albums.

Boston deejay Bob Crane arrived in LA in 1956 to host the KNX radio morning show. "The King of the Los Angeles

Airwaves" filled the second-story broadcast booth with his drum set, movie stars, and humor. His revolutionary show was the number-one rated morning show in Los Angeles and drew guests such as Marilyn Monroe, Ronald Reagan, Jayne Mansfield, Bob Hope, and Frank Sinatra, to name just a few. Crane, however, dreamed of becoming a star himself and it was during his reign at KNX that he captured the attention of CBS television executives. He began making guest appearances many CBS shows, including *The Dick Van Dyke Show,* and soon landed himself a regular role on *The Donna Reed Show* as Doctor David Kelsey. Crane's character was dropped after two seasons because executives decided the flirtatious Kelsey, was "too suggestive." Crane eventually left his $150,000-a-year position at KNX in 1965 to take the lead in a new CBS series, *Hogan's Heroes*, one of the most successful sitcoms of all time.

After *Hogan's Heroes* was canceled in 1971, Crane continued to act, appearing in two Disney films and made numerous guest appearances on TV shows *like Police Woman, Quincy,* and *The Love Boat*. He had his own TV show, *The Bob Crane Show,* in 1975, but it was canceled by NBC after just three months.

On Wednesday, June 28, 1978, after completing an evening theater performance in Arizona and signing autographs for fans in the lobby, Crane was murdered in his apartment. Some say it was his longtime friend, John Carpenter, who bludgeoned Crane to death, but John Carpenter died in 1998, maintaining his innocence to the very end. The full truth of the unsolved murder will probably never be known but it's good to know that Bob Crane chooses to return to KNX from time to time; a place where he probably spent the happiest years of his life.

William Paley stayed beyond CBS' compulsory retirement age of sixty-five, and sought to delay his inevitable passing of control to others. He worked through several short-lived potential heirs in the late 1970s, then stepped down as chief executive officer in 1977, but retained the powerful chairmanship. Finally, he hired Pillsbury's Thomas H. Wyman to become president in 1980. Wyman succeeded Paley as the network's second chairman in 1983. Concerned with some of Wyman's decisions in the aftermath of an unsuccessful attempt by Ted Turner to acquire CBS in 1985, Paley allied himself with Lawrence Tisch (by then holding the largest single block of company shares) to oust Wyman and install Tisch as chief executive officer in 1986. Paley returned as a figurehead chair until his death in late 1990, but by all accounts, he was still keeping an eye on the facility, in spirit, up until 2006 when KNX moved out of Columbia Square because the building had fallen into disrepair and asbestos problems were cited as a reason to demolish the historical broadcasting venue.

In August 2006, the property was acquired by Las Vegas-based developer Molasky Pacific LLC, for $66 million. They plan to redevelop the 125,000-square-foot complex to continue to attract entertainment industry tenants. Helmi Hisserich, regional administrator for the City of Los Angeles' Community Redevelopment Agency says redevelopment of Columbia Square will provide new housing, office and entertainment uses "while preserving the key historical elements of the property." The National Trust for Historic Preservation and Los Angeles Conservancy have been actively engaged in efforts to preserve the Hollywood landmark.

I recently spoke briefly to parapsychologist Dr. Larry Montz who heads up ISPR (The International Society for Paranormal Research). While he wasn't forthcoming with any details, he did admit that he and his team had recently investigated the location and says that while the building may currently be vacant to the naked eye, it is still filled to the rafters with the ghosts.

Hollywood's Ghostly Urban Legends

By definition, urban legends are classified as contemporary tall tales that emerge from the underground and take on colorful lives of their own. Often times there is no way of proving or disproving them, but in many instances, these stories are true. Here are just a few of Hollywood's best.

The Original Spanish Kitchen

This former restaurant at 7373 Beverly Boulevard in the Fairfax district is located just across the street from the famed El Coyote Restaurant and has become the subject of an urban legend which started in the early 1960s.

The restaurant, which opened in the mid-1940s, was a popular eating spot until September 1961, when the Original Spanish Kitchen closed for good. The closing of the restaurant was unusual because financially it was doing quite well, but stranger yet was the fact that the building's contents were left totally intact for years afterward. The tables continued to be set with full place settings and the lunch counter was fully stocked with coffee makers and cooking utensils. The sudden closure of the restaurant gave rise to speculation and the subsequent urban legend that the owners, who lived in an apartment above the restaurant, were murdered at the hands of organized crime, though this was never verified.

Over the years, reports of a haunting in the empty restaurant were quite common. Finally, after nearly forty years in limbo, the building is now the site of Privé, Laurent Duforg's upscale beauty salon. The Spanish Kitchen's original vertical electric sign, which had become a Los Angeles landmark was modified to read "SPA," a reference to the new business at the location.

The Amusement Park Mummy

During the filming of an episode of *The Six Million Dollar Man* in 1977 at a Long Beach amusement park known as The Pike, the show become associated with the creepiest of legends. The Long Beach Pike was considered to be the West Coast's Coney Island and featured some of the worlds most innovative rides and roller coasters. The venue began as a beach and bath house resort and was located at the end of the very fashionable red car electric line from Los Angeles.

Crowds came from all parts of the country to enjoy the beautiful beaches, the bath house, and the pool. On July 4, 1902, The Pike had been transformed into a real old-fashioned amusement park with games and thrill rides that fit every age group. Also known as the "Walk of a Thousand Lights," it became one of the most popular amusement parks on the west coast. After World War II, it was expanded and renamed Nu-Pike.

As the years passed, the park kept pace with newer and more modern rides, but it still retained its old-fashioned air of the country carnival with fun for all, and with no admission fee. During its heyday, the Pike's midway was filled with arcades, shooting galleries, cotton candy, hot dogs, cafes, and a Ripleys Believe It or Not type side show. The park officially shut down in 1969, but the location was often used as a favorite shooting location for movies and television shows. It was during one of those location shoots that Nu-Pike became famous for something even scarier than their rickety and terrifying 1930s era wooden roller coaster, The Cyclone Racer.

When the *Six Million Dollar Man* crew was setting up for a scene in the Laff-in-the-Dark ride, a technician tried to move a strange looking wax-covered mannequin hanging from a rope. When he did, the mannequin's arm broke off in his hand and sticking out of the wax shoulder socket was a large bone.

A doctor on the set was called over to have a look and he identified the grisly finding as a human bone. Los Angeles Chief Medical Examiner, Thomas Noguchi, was immediately called to investigate. Noguchi was known as the "coroner to the stars," and determined the cause of death in many high profile cases including Marilyn Monroe, Robert F. Kennedy, Janis Joplin, Albert Dekker, William Holden, John Belushi, Natalie Wood, and Sharon Tate.

The body was picked up by Los Angeles Coroner's Office, and after forensic scientists unclothed the figure and cut through the thick, hard wax surrounding it, they found that the body was indeed human. When the medical examiner opened the corpse's mouth for other clues, he was surprised to find a 1924 penny, the copper jacket of the bullet that killed the man, and a ticket from the Museum of Crime in Los Angeles.

Once the story got out, Noguchi received documents and photographs from Oklahoma Territorial Museum officials who believed the corpse was that of Oklahoma bad man Elmer McCurdy, a bank robber killed in a gunfight in 1911. His body had been embalmed with arsenic and sold to a traveling carnival show.

For the next sixty years, McCurdy's body was passed along to numerous wax museums, carnivals, and haunted houses. The owner of a haunted house near Mount Rushmore, South Dakota, refused to purchase it because he thought that McCurdy's body was actually a mannequin and wasn't lifelike enough. Eventually, the corpse wound up in the funhouse at the Long Beach Pike.

Noguchi set out to prove the museum's claims that the corpse was indeed McCurdy by using what he called "medical superimposition," comparing X-rays of the mummy's head with 1911 photographs taken by the mortuary. He also matched a tiny scar on the right wrist.

Once positive identification was made, Elmer McCurdy's remains were sent to Summit View Cemetery in Guthrie, Oklahoma, for a proper burial. Out of respect, some of the *Six Million Dollar Man* crew members attended his funeral.

The Oklahoma state medical examiner ordered that two cubic yards of concrete be poured over McCurdy's casket to insure that this much-traveled mummy could never be passed around again.

Griffith Park is Not Only Cursed, But Haunted!

Griffith Park at 4730 Crystal Springs Drive in the Los Feliz area of Los Angeles is a mix of wilderness, cultural sites, horse and hiking trails, and recreational facilities set on more than 4,000 acres in the hills between Hollywood and the San Fernando Valley.

In 1863, wealthy landowner Don Antonio Feliz died a horrible death from smallpox. Don Antonio, a bachelor, lived with his sister, a housekeeper named Soledad, and his niece, Petranilla. As smallpox was bringing an end to Don Antonio's life, nineteen-year-old Petranilla was sent away to protect her from the deadly and contagious disease. Soledad stayed on.

On his deathbed, Don Antonio was visited by an influential acquaintance, Don Antonio Coronel, and a lawyer, Don Innocante. The two visitors drew up the dying man's will and Innocante read it aloud. One version of the story says Feliz pronounced the will "all right." Another version claims a stick was fastened to the back of the dying man's head, forcing him to nod his ascent. In the end, Don Coronel was willed the rancho, Soledad got some furniture, and Petranilla got nothing.

Soledad was glad for her token inheritance, but Petranilla, who returned to find Coronel in control of the place she called home, would not accept her fate even though Coronel tried to use his persuasive powers to gracefully explain his sudden windfall. Petranilla would not be placated and this is when she unleashed the Feliz curse:

> *"Your falsity shall be your ruin! The substance of the Feliz family shall be your curse! The lawyer that assisted you in your infamy, and the judge, shall fall beneath the same curse! The one shall die an untimely death, the other in blood and violence! You, senor, shall know misery in your age and although you die rich, your substance shall go to vile persons! A blight shall fall upon the face of this terrestrial paradise, the cattle shall no longer fatten but sicken on its pastures, the fields shall no longer respond to the toil of the tiller, the grand oaks shall wither and die! The wrath of heaven and the vengeance of hell shall fall upon this place."*

Soon after, Don Coronel, for reasons best known to himself (some say that members of his family began dying grisly deaths), soon ceded the entire property to his lawyer but the lawyer was shot and killed shortly thereafter while celebrating the sale of the land's water rights.

The rancho was then sold to Leon "Lucky" Baldwin, who apparently spared no expense in trying to make it the most profitable and luxurious rancho in all of California, but Lucky Baldwin was not so lucky with this property either. The cattle sickened and died in the fields, his dairy business was a disastrous failure, fire destroyed the ripening grain, and grasshoppers wiped out the green crops. His vineyard was stricken with a strange blight, and finally Baldwin was forced to sell the rancho to pay off its mortgage.

Misfortune continued when the next owner, eccentric gold miner Colonel Griffith J. Griffith, who tried to make a go of the rancho, was plagued by droughts, fires, and other disasters. A violent storm in March 1884 brought lightning down upon the oaks. Waves of water cascaded down the hills onto the flatland. Ranch hands claimed they saw the ghost of Antonio Feliz riding the waves, later reappearing to dance the El Jarabe over the ruin that had been wrought. Others claim it was the ghost of Petranilla who was drifting about, renewing her curse.

Workers claimed a spirit calling itself Antonio Feliz sometimes appeared to them at a promontory in the park known as Bee Rock. Ostriches, which were being raised on the rancho, inexplicably stampeded at night. As the story goes, Griffith himself was so frightened by what was happening on his land that he would only visit the property at midday.

Griffith would eventually bestow the land to the City of Los Angeles as a "gift," but some say that this was just a desperate attempt to separate himself from the cursed land. However, it didn't work. His trying to give the land away merely aggravated the curse of Petronilla once again, because during the process, Griffith went a little bit crazy.

During a hotel stay in nearby Santa Monica, the Colonel botched an apparent homicide attempt on his dear wife. If it wasn't for the fact that Mrs. Griffith jerked her head at the last minute, she would have been dead. Instead, she took a bullet to the eye and lived to testify at her husband's murder trial. "It was deliberate," she testified. "He made me get down on my knees and handed me a prayer book." The shooting left Christina Griffith disfigured and blind in one eye, and an author who attended Griffith's trial dubbed Christina Griffith as "the society wife who wouldn't die." Colonel Griffith was sentenced to two years in prison then returned to Los Angeles where he remained for the remaining thirteen years of his life.

Whether the curse still exists today is anybody's guess, but Griffith Park has consistently had its share of disasters. On October 3, 1933, 3,780 men hired as part of a welfare project, were in the park clearing brush when fire broke out in the Mineral Wells area. Many of the workers volunteered or were ordered to fight the fire, and a foremen with no knowledge of fire fighting, directed the effort, setting inappropriate backfires and sending hundreds of workers into a steep canyon. When the wind changed direction, they were trapped. In all, 29 men were killed and 150 were injured. When professional firefighters arrived, they were able to limit the blaze to 47 acres, but because of the disorganized nature of the employment, it took weeks to establish the exact death toll and identify the bodies. The Griffith Park fire remains the deadliest in Los Angeles history.

In 2006, Griffith Park was put on alert when L.A. County's Acute Communicable Disease Control Unit issued a bubonic plague alert after a park visitor was found to have contracted — and survived — a bout with the Black Death. Some people speculate that the curse is losing its edge and that Petronilla's spirit is being appeased by the numerous bodies that are frequently dumped at the park — sacrifices perhaps?

On May 8, 2007, Griffith Park suffered yet another devastating fire which burned more than 600 acres and threatened many of the park's famous venues. The Los Angeles Zoo, Gene Autry's Museum of the American West, the world renowned Greek Theater, and The Griffith Observatory all had to be evacuated. Dozens of homes in the area were threatened as well. The fire began around one o'clock in the afternoon and by nine o'clock at night, blazing firestorms were bursting all over the park area lighting up the night sky with bright orange towers of flames. This was the fifth blaze in the park since December 2006, and the largest, and most destructive fire since 1961. At this writing, its cause is still under investigation. Los Angeles Mayor Antonio Villaraigosa was quoted as saying that there were "no facts to indicate that this is an arson fire … it could be an accident." But was it really an accident, or was Petaonilla at it again?

Ghost hunters claim that Griffith Park is indeed haunted and the rumors are too plentiful to ignore. Sightings include a

Yankee horseman, a bearded man who travels briskly on foot, a group of mission Indians who appear to be on the run, a Mexican outlaw, a Spanish don, Col. Griffith J. Griffith who appears on horseback and, of course, Petranilla Feliz herself. She appears as a pale partial apparition of a short Hispanic woman dressed in a flowing white gown.

There is also the legend of a haunted picnic table within the park. The table is supposedly possessed by the ghosts of two young lovers who were crushed to death "in flagrante delicto" by a falling tree back in 1976. It is said that their cremated remains were scattered upon the location where the childhood sweethearts died in each others' arms. Witnesses claim that strange things began to happen in that area shortly after their deaths and purportedly continue to occur to this day, especially around the anniversary of their passing. It is said that the two unfortunate lovebirds are never far away from the picnic table that both brought them together and tore them apart.

A few years after the couple died, a Griffith Park tree trimmer swears that a newly-felled tree he was working on started bouncing up and down all by itself on the fateful picnic table. Then he heard moaning and crying and got so scared he ran to his truck. Once inside the cab, a very sinister voice whispered in his ear, "Leave us alone!"

In 2002, a former Griffith Park ranger also claims to have encountered the ghosts. It was late at night and he was driving past the picnic table area when out of nowhere he heard an unearthly noise from somewhere up in the brush to the north. He said it started as a horrible sobbing that alternated between screams and a wicked laugh that made the hair on the back of his neck stand straight up. Then he saw what looked to be two shrouded figures with glowing red eyes running into the brush.

Armed with just a flashlight, he got out of the truck and gave chase. The screaming stopped abruptly when he was not more than a few feet past the table. Everything was quiet until he was suddenly overcome with a deep sense of dread and evil and that's when the ranger's flashlight failed.

He tried running back to his truck but felt like he was suddenly enveloped in a suffocating embrace, there was freezing cold air on his neck and he felt as if something grabbed him around his chest. Then a voice whispered "Leave us alone!" accompanied by what he described as "the smell of death." Then he passed out.

The ranger filed no report on the incident, but put in for a transfer first thing the next day because after going home and unbuttoning his shirt the night before, his chest was caked with dried blood with a warning scratched into it as if with a fingernail. It read: "Next time you die."

Haunted Bronson Canyon

Once known as Brush Canyon, Bronson Canyon is located on the western side of Griffith Park and is well known for the numerous movies and television shows that have been filmed in the area since the early 1920s. In recent years, this remote wilderness setting has been used as a location for shows like *Bonanza, Star Trek,* and *Little House on the Prairie.* The canyon is in constant use making it one of the most important location sites in motion picture history.

The Union Rock Company, who began quarrying crushed rock in the canyon to be used for railroad ballast and for surfacing streets in 1903, inadvertently created one of the most recognized movie locations in Bronson Canyon. When they ceased operation in the 1920s, they left behind a man made hole in the mountain that soon became known as The Bronson Caves, probably most widely recognized as the "Bat Cave" in the classic 1960s television series, *Batman.*

Information about Bronson Canyon ghosts isn't easy to come by from those in the know. While Griffith Park Rangers do not deny that the canyon is haunted, and even hinted at a scary incident that took place at the nearby Girl's Camp a few years ago, I was told by the ranger's office that they are "not allowed to tell ghost stories." If there weren't stories to tell, then why the gag order?

Hikers who venture into the area after dark are often spooked by stories about the tragic death of stuntman Jack Tyree, who was killed during the filming of the movie *The Sword and The Sorcerer* in 1981 when he jumped off a cliff and missed his airbag.

Because of that tragic incident, as well as the hundreds of productions that have been filmed there, and the haunted history of Griffith Park itself, one must assume that Bronson Canyon is indeed haunted.

Peg Entwhistle Haunts the Hollywood Sign

The world famous Hollywood Sign on the southern side of Mt. Lee in the Hollywood Hills was erected in 1924 as an advertisement for a real estate venture called "Hollywood-land." The development was announced in the Los Angeles Times as "one of the most attractive residential sections of the City of Los Angeles."

The real estate syndicate was comprised of General M. H. Sherman (founder of West Hollywood), Harry Chandler (Publisher of the *L. A. Times*) and developer Sidney H. Wood-ruff. Their grand vision for Hollywoodland was to develop a Mediterranean Riviera in the Hollywood Hills between Griffith Park and Lake Hollywood. With architecture and landscaping inspired by the southern regions of France, Italy, and Spain, Hollywoodland was marketed to wealthy winter visitors to Los Angeles from the East Coat. New Englanders could select their hillside lot and architectural style then find their new home waiting for them the following season, fully built and landscaped by the developers. Hollywoodland became

America's first themed residential community and much of the attention and press coverage was due to a huge sign reading "Hollywoodland" which crowned Beachwood Canyon. The original Hollywoodland sign was built out of sheet metal and telephone poles at a cost of $21,000. The sign was covered with 4,000 flashing electric light bulbs which could be seen as far away as Long Beach harbor on a clear evening.

Hollywoodland's real estate development experienced a slide in the 1930s due to the 1929 stock market crash, and by the 1940s, the developers were no longer able to pay anyone to maintain the sign. It was abandoned and left derelict until 1949 when the *H* toppled over in the wind. The Hollywood Chamber of Commerce then stepped in and offered to remove the last four letters of the sign and repair the rest. Today, the Hollywood Sign has the distinction of being one of the most famous and recognizable signs in the entire world, but back in 1932, the landmark made headlines for being a prop in one of Hollywood's most famous suicides.

By all accounts, actress Peg Entwistle was fascinated by the glittering Hollywood sign, and she lived in the canyon right below it with her uncle Harold at 2428 Beachwood Drive.

Peg had emigrated to New York City from Wales with her widower father when she was a child of fourteen. The young girl had stars in her eyes, but after her father was hit and killed by a car, she experienced the first of many depressive episodes that she was to suffer throughout her short life.

In spite of her emotional pain, Peg followed her dream and became an actress, appearing in several Broadway shows. While working on Broadway, she met and fell in love with a fellow actor named Robert Keith. He was a popular star and despite his being ten years Peg's senior, the two soon fell in love and got married. But the marriage quickly soured because during a visit to her mother-in-law's house, Peg noticed a photograph of a young boy on the mantel. She asked who he was and was informed that he was Robert's son from his first marriage, a fact that he had kept hidden from her. (That surprise stepson was future actor Brian Keith, star of the television show *Family Affair*.)

Weeks later, during a dinner party at their home, a policeman came to the door and demanded nearly $1,000 in back child support that Robert owed. Peg managed to get the money together, but when she asked Robert about it, he became violent and the couple was soon divorced.

Peg then felt that it was time for a fresh start and did what most young hopefuls did at the time — she moved to Hollywood.

Once she got here, Peg found work in small theater. Her first production was a play called *Mad Hopes*, starring Billie Burke, who would go on to play Glenda the good witch in *The Wizard of Oz*, and another Hollywood newcomer named Humphrey Bogart. The play opened to decent reviews, but only lasted a week and a half. Peg saw it as another personal failure, but because of her good looks and her popularity on Broadway, Peg landed a short-term contract with RKO Studios and was cast in a small part in the film *Thirteen Women*. She knew that even though it was a small part, it would lead to other offers. But when the film bombed at the box office, the studio dropped her contract and Peg's dreams of stardom began to fade. This pushed her into such a severe depression and she completely gave up her dream of becoming a big Hollywood star.

One September evening in 1932, Peg left the house, telling her uncle she was going to the drugstore and then would be visiting friends. Instead, she hiked up the canyon to the dirt fire road that accessed the Hollywood sign. When she got to the letter H, Peg climbed up the back of the sign using a workman's ladder that had been left behind and then jumped to her death. She left a note in her purse saying, "I am afraid, I am a coward. I am sorry for everything. If I had done this a long time ago, it would have saved a lot of pain. P.E."

The next morning, a hiker found her broken body at the bottom of the sign and reported it to the police. The *Los Angeles Times* got wind of the tragedy and dubbed the nameless girl "The Hollywood Sign Girl." They published her suicide note in the hopes that she would be identified. Her uncle recognized the initials and identified her body in the morgue. Peg was cremated and her ashes interred in her father's grave at Oak Hill Cemetery in Glendale, Ohio.

The eeriest part of the suicide was its bad timing, because shortly after Peg's death, a letter from the Beverly Hills Playhouse arrived at her Uncle Harold's home. The Playhouse wanted to star Peg in their next production which ironically was about a young woman driven to suicide.

Some say the mournful ghost of Peg Entwistle still haunts the base of the sign where her body was discovered. Reports of her weeping ghost continue to this day. Park rangers and hikers in the area often describe seeing a young blonde woman dressed in old-fashioned clothing who vanishes when approached. Others have reported the strong scent of gardenias in the area. The gardenia scent was known to be Peg's trademark perfume. In recent years, alarms systems have been installed near the Hollywood sign to keep people away from it because there is always a danger of vandals... and suicides. The alarm systems incorporate the use of motion detectors and lights to keep intruders away. One park ranger recalled a number of times when the alarm system stated that someone was close to the sign, even though a check by the ranger revealed no one was there. "There have been times when I have been at the sign," he said, "and the motion detectors say that someone is standing five feet away from me... only there's nobody there." He also went on to say that Peg normally makes her presence known very late at night, especially when it is foggy, and always in the vicinity of the Hollywood sign.

Walt Disney on Ice

In the decades since Walt Disney's death, the claim that he arranged for his body to be frozen has been repeated over and over again. Nearly everyone familiar with the name *Walt Disney* has heard the story that his corpse is stored in a deep-freeze chamber in an undisclosed location. The most frequently mentioned site of the entombment is directly under Disneyland's "Pirates of the Caribbean" attraction. It is supposedly there awaiting the day when science can repair the damage to his body and bring "Uncle Walt" back to life. While there is no documented evidence to suggest that Walt Disney was interested in, or had even heard of cryonics before his passing, Disney's ghost is still very much alive, and rumor has it that he spends quite a bit of time at the Magic Kingdom he so lovingly created.

It was Disney's vision to create a place where children and parents could have fun together. The more Walt dreamed of a magical park, the more imaginative and elaborate it became. Walt planned out all the lands to the finest detail. Main Street, U.S.A., at the very front of the park, was where Walt wanted his guests to relive the typical turn-of-the-century city life and it's on Main Street where he built himself an apartment right above the Main Street Fire Station because he wanted a place to stay and watch the activity during the park's construction.

After the park opened, the apartment, which was private and hidden from the rest of Disneyland, was the perfect place for Walt to do quiet work, or enjoy time with his family. And whenever he needed to get downstairs in a hurry, he often used the station's brass fire pole instead of taking the stairs.

The apartment was very small, only about 500 square feet in size, but fully operational and decorated in the Victorian theme to match its surroundings on Main Street. The apartment also featured a quiet patio where Lillian Disney often had her afternoon tea and entertained guests.

When Walt was in residence, there was a small lamp in the window that was always turned on. Today that lamp remains on all the time in Walt's memory. Some say it is kept on to remind people that Walt's spirit is still there, because some employees claim to hear foot steps in the apartment late at night when nobody is there and also hear knocking on the door. Others believe that Disney's ghost moves around the park quite a bit in order to keep a watchful eye on things. And according to numerous reports, he doesn't seem to be the only ghost at the park.

In The Christmas Shop, some employees report a strange feeling when alone. There is an old photo from the nineteenth century of a young woman up on one of the shelves, and it has been documented several times that the photo of the woman will change expression from time to time accompanied by a strange wind in the room. The Haunted Mansion supposedly has three resident spirits. In the It's a Small World ride, lights turn themselves on and off and the dolls suddenly begin moving by themselves when the power is turned off. In The Star Trader store's stock room people have felt a cold, eerie wind — this is cause for alarm because there are no doors, vents, or windows up there.

The Matterhorn is said to be haunted by the ghost of a woman named Dolly who was crushed to death after she fell out of her sled and was hit by the sled behind her. In Space Mountain both the ride itself and the women employees' locker rooms are haunted by the ghost of "Mr. One-Way," a guest who died on the Space Mountain ride back in the 1970s. On the ride, he is described as a large man with reddish hair and a red face, and has been seen by guests getting into a car with a lone rider, but he vanishes before the end of the ride.

There are several other reported Disneyland hauntings, but of all the locations in the park, The Disney Gallery, which is above the Pirates of the Caribbean ride, seems to be the place where the ghost of Walt Disney himself is most often seen. Workers have reported that after park closing and in the early morning hours, they see a figure of a tall man walking around in the Gallery which they believe to be Disney.

Los Angeles Pet Cemetery

The memorial park at 5068 N. Old Scandia Lane in Calabasas was founded in 1928, making it one of the oldest facilities of its kind on the West Coast. One historical feature of note is the brick mausoleum, which was erected in 1929, and is the oldest original structure on the property. There is also a gravestone at the cemetery marked "The Rainbow Bridge." Its inscription is both comforting, and at the same time, a grim reminder that one day we will all be crossing that bridge to the other side. It reads:

Just this side of heaven is a place called Rainbow Bridge.

When an animal dies that has been especially close to someone here, that pet goes to Rainbow Bridge.

There are meadows and hills for all of our special friends so they can run and play together.

There is plenty of food, water and sunshine, and our friends are warm and comfortable.

All the animals who had been ill and old are restored to health and vigor; those who were hurt or maimed are made whole and strong again, just as we remember them in our dreams of days and times gone by.

The animals are happy and content, except for one small thing; they each miss someone very special to them, who had to be left behind.

They all run and play together, but the day comes when one suddenly stops and looks into the distance. His bright eyes are intent; His eager body quivers.

Suddenly he begins to run from the group, flying over the green grass, his legs carrying him faster and faster.

You have been spotted, and when you and your special friend finally meet, you cling together in joyous reunion, never to be parted again. The happy kisses rain upon your face; your hands again caress the beloved head, and you look once more into the trusting eyes of your pet, so long gone from your life but never absent from your heart.

Then you cross Rainbow Bridge together...

—Author Unknown

The Los Angeles Pet Cemetery is where, for decades, many Hollywood stars have buried their beloved pets. The Little Rascal's dog Petey, Hopalong Cassidy's Horse, and Mary Pickford's dog are all interred here. However, the ghost that does the most haunting at the cemetery is Kabar, a Great Dane that belonged to Rudolf Valentino. The dog died in 1929, but its friendly, playful spirit is still greeting people with a lick on their hand when they wander near his grave.

The Haunting of Wattles Mansion

The Wattles Mansion is a Hollywood residence in the Mission Revival style that was built in 1907 at 1824 N. Curson Avenue by Myron Hunt and Elmer Grey, architects of the Huntington Art Gallery and the Pasadena Library. The house was built as the winter home of Omaha banker Gurdon Wattles. A garden enthusiast, Wattles is said to have been deliriously happy with L.A.'s balmy climate because it enabled him to have a garden that bloomed year-round. He regularly changed the landscaping of his entire estate. Some vintage photos show a Spanish garden with cypress trees lining the terraces; others depict an abundance of tropical vegetation.

After Wattles' death, his estate fell into disrepair and was sold to the City of Los Angeles. It wasn't until 1983 that the preservationist group Hollywood Heritage, Inc. began restoring the mansion and grounds. Through their efforts, the Wattles Mansion has been returned to its former splendor, but it seems as though several loud spirits, both man and beast sometimes disturb the mansion's tranquil surroundings.

There used to be a bus stop right in front of the property, but it had to be moved because there were many complaints of screaming, and mysterious sounds of horses galloping and whinnying all night long. An apparition of a woman has also been seen roaming the grounds at night.

The Charlie Chaplin Mansion

This affluent house sits upon a hill overlooking Echo Park in a neighborhood called Hathaway Hills. According to legend, Charlie Chaplin used to own the property, and after he sold it, a man moved in with his family. Shortly thereafter, the man went insane and murdered his entire family.

As the story goes, he came home from work one afternoon and proceeded to kill his mother, his wife, and his children. People who have visited the home describe it as being a very depressing. It has been reported that one can see the ghost of the grandmother and hear the children screaming. There have been other reports of eerie sounds and sightings of wild animals. The house is an old Victorian style and resembles the *Psycho* house of movie fame.

Lon Chaney Haunts Universal Studios

Lon Chaney, nicknamed "The Man of a Thousand Faces," started his career during the silent film era and was one of the most versatile and powerful character actors of his time. The actor was so well-respected in the industry that when he died on August 26, 1930, every studio in Hollywood observed two minutes of silence while a squad of Marines lowered the MGM flag. Fellow character actor Wallace Beery flew his plane over the funeral and dropped wreaths of flowers.

Chaney is best remembered for his characterizations of tortured, often grotesque and afflicted characters, as well as for his groundbreaking artistry with film makeup. Chaney is chiefly remembered as a pioneer in such horror films as (the silent versions of) *The Hunchback of Notre Dame* and most notably *The Phantom of the Opera*. Chaney's son, Lon Chaney, Jr., was also known for acting in horror movies. Most remember him as *The Wolf Man* but he was also featured in many other films not in the horror genre including the 1939 feature film version of *Of Mice and Men*, in which he played Lennie Small and received critical acclaim.

The Chaneys recently appeared on U. S. postage stamps as their signature characters of the *Phantom of the Opera* and the *Wolf Man*, with the set rounded out by Bela Lugosi as *Dracula* and Boris Karloff as Frankenstein's monster and *The Mummy*.

Universal Studios, the studio that brought movie audiences some of the scariest horror movies of all time, had Chaney under contract from 1912 through 1917 doing bit or character parts. He returned to the studio in 1924 to make *Phantom of the Opera* on Stage 28. The massive opera house set was so gigantic that construction was started a year before the actual production began and it has gone on to become a permanent fixture on the Universal lot.

Visitors and employees to Stage 28 have long maintained that it is haunted. For many years, there have been sightings by electricians, designers, carpenters, and security guards of a man in a black cape who seems to come and go without warning. Those who have gotten more than just a glimpse of him say that the cloaked man is Lon Chaney himself. Many visitors who do not know the history of Stage 28 have also reported catching a glimpse of the man in the black cape. He is often seen running on the catwalks overhead. Even security guards who have laughed off the idea of a resident ghost admit to being "spooked" by lights that turn on and off by themselves and by doors that open and close on the empty stage at night. There are also reports that a huge chandelier, which was removed from the original set years ago, seems to have a life of its own and tinkles at people who pass by it every so often.

Universal Studios are located at 3900 Lankershim Boulevard in Burbank.

Haunted Hollywood Schools

The Hollywood High playing field, home of The Sheiks.

Hollywood High School

Schools are always filled with lots of energy and my old alma mater, Hollywood High School, located at 1521 N. Highland Avenue is no different.

The school was established in 1903 and by the 20s, it became the school of choice for the children of movie stars and future movie stars as well. Fay Wray, James Garner, and John Ritter are just a few of the school's illustrious alumni who have gone on to become famous Hollywood stars.

Over the years, it has grown into the most well known and one of the most notable high schools in America. The school mascot and team name is The Sheiks, which was derived from silent film actor Rudolph Valentino, who in 1921 became a great star with the release of The Sheik. When a local sportswriter dubbed the team with its world famous moniker, the name stuck. The school newspaper, *The Sheik Press* debuted in 1917. Almost 100 percent of all issues published still exist and one of the most celebrated editors of the Sheik Press was Carol Burnett, Class of 1951.

In addition to being famous for it's celebrated alumni, Hollywood High is also famous for its Performing Arts Department and many a dramatic review has been performed in the famous school's auditorium. But along with the onstage drama, throughout the years there has also been quite of bit of commotion going on behind the scenes, some of which has resulted in ghostly activity within its hallowed walls.

The school's pool area is said to be haunted by an unfortunate student who slipped, struck his head, and died on the spot. The boys' locker room, the performing arts center, and the library all seem to be haunted as well. A ghostly woman was contacted during a brief séance in the school library, and at one point, the spirits of a former student and actor John Ritter were said to come through.

One spirit who also paid them a visit was that of a former teacher urging who he thought were students to continue to rehearse for the next school play. Many teachers and students have reported hearing doors open and close by them selves, loud hammering, objects moved from one place to another, a shadow roaming around in the auditorium where he hung himself.

There are supposedly three ghosts that haunt the school. The first is a young boy that goes by the name of Toby who committed suicide after his girlfriend left him for someone else. Another young man reportedly drowned in the pool and has been seen walking around the gym hall and pool. The third entity is that of a drama teacher who taught at the school for well over thirty years.

Bancroft Middle School

Bancroft Middle School, at 929 N. Las Palmas Avenue has been teaching Hollywood kids since 1929. Ricky Nelson, Judy Garland, and Brandy are just a few of the school's former celebrity students. Located just a short block away from Hollywood Center Studios, the school has gone through an extensive renovation since the 1971 Sylmar and the 1992 Northridge earthquakes. Some of the tearing down and rebuilding might have shaken up a few ghosts. Late at night and early in the morning, teachers and students claim to hear whispers and footsteps behind them in the main building when nobody is there. Also, in the school gym, lights suddenly go on and off by themselves, the climbing ropes will start to quiver, and the volleyball nets start to shake on their own.

Melrose Elementary School

Melrose Elementary School, located at 731 N. Detroit Street in West Hollywood, is said to be haunted by the ghost of a janitor who hung himself in the auditorium because he thought nobody liked him. Since then his ghost has been seen roaming the stage and the halls. At times, all the curtains start to move by themselves. Some students and teachers hear scratches on the door during class, but don't find anyone there when they go to check. The scratching noises also occur in one of the ladies restrooms and the door begins to shake by itself.

Fairfax High School

At Fairfax High School, located at 7850 Melrose Avenue in the Fairfax District, shadows have been seen and cold spots have been felt in the rotunda area. Two people have supposedly committed suicide there, one by hanging and the other by jumping off the rotunda. A number of students have claimed that they felt the urge to jump off the third floor balcony for no apparent reason. Cold spots have also been felt in various areas of the school and lights flicker on and off in the auditorium. It's been rumored that one person died in a fall while trying to fix the lights.

Ozzie and Harriet's House

Ghosts and hauntings are probably the last thing that comes to mind when you think of the perpetually cheerful Ozzie and Harriet Nelson, but Ozzie, for years America's favorite father, reportedly haunts his old Hollywood Hills home. Ozzie may not be very content in the afterlife because family members have seen Ozzie's ghost in the house and he always appears to be in a somber mood.

The Nelsons bought the house at 1822 Camino Palmero in 1941, and the family lived there for nearly forty years. Ozzie Nelson, who created, directed, produced, and co-wrote the popular television sitcom *The Adventures of Ozzie and Harriet,* which aired from 1952 to 1966, was everybody's favorite TV dad. The show portrayed a fictionalized version of the Nelson's family life at home and the exterior of the television house is said to have been an exact replica of the real-life Nelson home.

After Ozzie passed away on June 3, 1975, Harriet continued to live in the house until 1980, and then put the home up for sale. While it's hard to imagine Ozzie Nelson as either grim or mischievous, subsequent owners of the property believe that Ozzie continues to remain in his beloved home and likes to make his presence known. New owners have experienced water faucets and lights that turn themselves on and off, doors that open and close by themselves, and loud footsteps when no one is there. One owner even tells a story that "someone" got fresh with her during the night when her blankets were pulled back and she felt someone kissing her neck and breasts.

Probably the most telling proof of spirit activity in the house came in the summer 1994 when the house was vacant. A painter had been hired to freshen the place up, and over time, he got used to hearing phantom footsteps walking around when he knew he was the only one in the house. But when he came face to face with a misty white form that resembled a human being, he was convinced that he had seen a ghost. He couldn't be sure if it was Ozzie, but he was certain that he'd had an "otherworldly" encounter.

Groucho Keeps Them Laughing

One of Groucho Marx's famous tag lines was, "…A likely story and probably true," so with that in mind, the story about Groucho haunting his old office above The Laugh Factory comedy club on the famed Sunset Strip does seem to have some merit.

The Laugh Factory, located at 8001 Sunset Boulevard is one of the best known comedy stages in the world and has been graced by such stars as Rodney Dangerfield, Richard Pryor, Robin Williams, Jerry Seinfeld, Chris Rock, and many more.

Groucho Marx had his business office on the second floor of the famed comedy club and, it seems he's still conducting business — in an ethereal sort of way. It has been reported that Groucho still makes nightly appearances in his old office. If you don't believe the rumors, just remember another of Groucho's famous quotes: "Who are you going to believe, me or your own eyes?"

Jayne Mansfield was Beheaded

Despite having a genius IQ of 163, stage and film star Jayne Mansfield, known for her roles as a dizzy sexpot, was never quite able to rid herself of the "dumb blond" image, so the sly-as-a-fox Jayne played into it and pulled many outrageous publicity stunts during her day, including "stranding" herself on a desert island. In her personal life, she was at one time married to body builder Mickey Hargitay and was a doting mother of four. In an interview in *Star Weekly* magazine, Jayne was quoted as saying, "We take our children everywhere we go. I don't believe in having them and then leaving them to someone else to bring up." And to that end, Jayne's children were with her on June 29, 1967, when the actress met her tragic end at the age of thirty-four.

En route to a television appearance in Louisiana with her boyfriend, divorce lawyer Sam Brody, their driver, and her three children with Hargitay the car, they rounded a curve on a dark stretch of road on U.S. Highway 90 in Mississippi and slammed into and underneath a slow-moving truck. Though the children survived with minor injuries, everyone sitting in the front was killed instantly.

When photographers snapped a shot of Jayne's blonde bouffant wig lying on the ground at the accident scene, it became contemporary lore that she had been decapitated. While her death was indeed gruesome, (her death certificate lists the cause of death as a "crushed skull with avulsion of the cranium and brain") she was not beheaded. She was "scalped."

...and the plot thickens...

Following her death, and with the decapitation story still raging, another tale began to circulate which gave speculation that the Devil himself might have had a hand in Jayne's premature demise.

It seems that Mansfield became involved with Anton LaVey and his Church of Satan in the mid sixties. Mansfield went to see LaVey because she wanted to put a curse on her ex- husband who was instigating a custody battle for the children. When the court decided in Jayne's favor, she became convinced that the satanic ritual had worked. Then, when her youngest son was mauled by a lion at an animal park, she sought out LaVey to perform a ritual to save her son. The boy soon recovered and Mansfield then dedicated herself to LaVey and the church. Mansfield's boyfriend, Sam Brody, was not too happy with his girlfriend's obsession with Satan and began threatening LaVey.

LaVey didn't take too kindly to the threats and proceeded to put a curse on Sam. In doing so, he also warned Mansfield to stay away from Brody so that none of the curse would rub of on her, but obviously Mansfield didn't listen.

LaVey would later come forward and take the blame for Mansfield's death. He claimed that while he was in the midst of his daily rituals, he stopped to clip some newspaper articles. After cutting out one particular article, he flipped it over to see what was on the other side, and there was a picture of Mansfield minus her head. He had inadvertently snipped it off. As the story goes, while he was reflecting on the headless image, the phone rang, and the caller passed on the news that Mansfield had just died.

Nicole Simpson's Haunted Condo

In 1994, O. J. Simpson's former wife, Nicole Brown Simpson and her friend Ronald Goldman were found savagely murdered outside her Brentwood townhouse. O. J. was arrested following a bizarre, sixty-mile, slow-speed police pursuit on the L.A. Freeway system. Ninety-five million people watched the freeway drama unfold on live television as Simpson headed back to his Brentwood home in a white Ford Bronco, holding a gun to his own head. Simpson claimed to be innocent of the crime, and after one of the longest and most-watched trials in history, he was found "not guilty" of all charges.

It should come as no surprise to anyone that the murder scene in Brentwood is reportedly haunted, but more than two years before Nicole's murder, the condominium next door to hers was "haunted" by the sound of a woman screaming and of heavy footsteps running away. At times the screams were so loud, neighbors called to see if everything was all right. One night, the residents were surprised when police knocked on the door claiming they'd received a 911 emergency call from a woman in the house. No one in the house had made the call. The family consulted a parapsychologist who tried to obtain the 911 tape from the police, but could not.

Just prior to the Simpson/Goldman murders, the sounds subsided but after Nicole's death, they returned with a vengeance. Coincidence? Not likely. Nicole's 911 calls were played to the masses including the sounds of a woman screaming and heavy footsteps running away. Déjà vu?

The Brown family put the condo up for sale shortly after the murders but it was too soon and the stigma too deep. Nobody wanted to live there, and the property sat empty for two-and-a-half years. Finally the place sold for $200,000 less than Nicole had paid for it. During the time it sat vacant, ghost hunters flocked to the ill-fated condo which quickly got the reputation for being haunted. People taking photographs on the property came up with spooky images that resembled both of the victims, especially in the tree leaves.

Boris Karloff's Personal Graveyard

This tale happens to be my personal favorite. According to legend, when he wasn't stomping around the *Frankenstein* set with bolts in his neck, Boris Karloff was an avid gardener. Apparently his old friends from the Vaudeville days liked his garden as much as he did, and when his cronies began to die off, several asked to be buried in his garden, so he did the honorable thing and complied with their last wishes and planted them one by one alongside his beloved rose bushes. 2320 Bowmont Drive in Beverly Hills 90210.

The Hollywood American Legion Hall

2035 N. Highland Avenue, Hollywood, California 90028

The Hollywood Post of the American Legion is known as the "Motion Picture Post," being comprised mainly of men connected with various branches of the film industry who served in the World War. From its inception in 1929, the 33,000 square foot Egyptian Revival-Moroccan Deco building that houses Hollywood American Legion Post 43 was the favorite haunt of local artists, film stars, and politicians. Humphrey Bogart was often seen and heard in the basement bar while Lana Turner, Rita Hayward, Shirley Temple, Jane Mansfield, and Marilyn Monroe were also frequents visitors in the 1930s and 40s. In recent years, quite a bit of paranormal activity has been associated with the hall and the ghostly sightings continue to this day.

A helpful ghost is often seen by TV and film crews who frequently use the venue for filming. He appears as a full-blown apparition and offers to help out with moving equipment, and then suddenly vanishes. In the stage area, one of the staff members who used to be an actor was practicing his "Julius Caesar" audition speech late one night. He was all alone in the building and when he was done rehearsing, he heard clapping from somewhere in the empty auditorium. Instead of sticking around for an encore, the frightened man immediately fled the building.

In the downstairs bar, a bartender was loading a few things into the elevator and twice saw an apparition during the process. The first time he thought he was just tired and his eyes might be playing tricks on him, but the second time the apparition appeared, it was more opaque and actually said, "Can I help you?" The bartender ran out, but not before he left a note saying that he was never coming back in the building.

Other visitors claim to have heard loud, unexplained banging noises and other strange sounds. Two locals were in the Atrium Room one night and heard what sounded like a man and woman laughing. They were more shocked than scared because the laughter sounded as if the man was playfully chasing the woman around the balcony.

When British medium David Wells visited the Hall with TV's *Most Haunted* crew in 2005, they also experienced quite a bit of ghostly activity. "There were echoes of the whole Marilyn Monroe/JFK affair throughout," said David. " I picked up their layers, not their presence. And there's a bar downstairs where all the movers and shakers used to gather and the air is very thick with it down there." Interestingly enough, the Hall was where Marilyn Monroe was first introduced to Hollywood at the start of her career.

David also connected with the spirit of Marshall, an elderly caretaker who had lived in the building and subsequently died by falling down a set of stairs just five years before. According to David, while Marshall seems to hang around quite a bit, he isn't grounded. "He seems to have crossed over and then comes back. We're all given free will when we pass," explained David, " and a lot of spirits don't cross because they have a choice. Marshall was very fond of his friend, Terry Duddy, who also works there, so Marshall would come back quite often, especially when he felt that Terry needed his support."

David also got the impression that Marshall had a definite agenda. "He had stuff lying around before he crossed over that was very damning. He knew a few secrets or some information he was trying to protect or bring to the fore. He wasn't just there because he loved the place, although he did, but he was also troubled and had a job to do.

"The thing I like about Marshall," said David, "is that his communication to me was very clear, almost as though he was talking in my ear. I could clearly make out his accent and the way he spoke.

When David asked Marshall to tell him something personal so that positive identification could be made, Marshall said, "Ask Terry about the naked story." When Terry heard that, there was no question that David was, in fact, communicating with Marshall's spirit because nobody knew about the embarrassing story but he and Marshall.

Terry went on to explain that early one morning, Marshall got up to go get the newspaper. Since nobody was around, Marshall didn't bother to put on any clothes but once he got outside, the door slammed shut behind him, and there he stood, in the buff, with no way of getting back in.

Marshall now seems to roam the whole building happily and is not shy about making his presence known. During *Most Haunted's* investigation of the bar, a television set mounted on the wall turned itself off repeatedly. In an effort to make sure that this phenomenon was not an electrical malfunction, the show's cast asked the spirit to turn the television set off and on when they prompted him to, and the spirit complied with his instructions each and every time.

As a séance was taking place in the bar, some of the cast members were sitting next door in the adjacent pool room. The séance participants asked for any spirit who happened to be there to try and move some of the balls on the pool table in the next room. At that moment the 8-ball literally jumped out of the pool table pocket and landed on the floor at the opposite end of the room, much to the shock of those who were sitting there watching it happen. When they asked for the spirit to again move the 8-ball it did indeed move. According to David, "It was Marshall who threw the pool balls."

Later on during the investigation, David came across another spirit in the building's small theater. "I couldn't get a fix on who it was, but when you walk into the theater, you hear applause…not from many, but a single person applauding, and it's not very enthusiastic applause at all. It was more like a *So what? Been there done that* sort of clapping rather than *Wow, that was great!*

"We then actually got up on the stage and started dancing about trying to elicit some sort of reaction from the seemingly bored spirit but unfortunately we didn't get any response," said David. When I was suggested that they were probably lucky that they didn't get anything thrown at them for their ad lib performance, David just laughed. "An astral tomato would have been lovely."

Curious to see if the American Legion Hall is still being haunted by Marshall or anyone else since *Most Haunted's* visit, I spoke to Terry Duddy and he confirmed David Wells' suspicion that the attempt to cross Marshall over to the other side had not worked out.

"We've had one incident since *Most Haunted* was here, and that was with a grip on a movie shoot. He was rolling cable and saw somebody walk into a room and he thought it was an extra who was dressed as a waiter. He dropped his cable and went to tell the person that they should get out of there because they were done shooting for the day. When he walked into the room there was nobody in there, and of course the only entrance and exit was the way he'd just walked in. He came to me and told me what happened and wondered what the hell was going on. So I took him downstairs and I pointed to a picture on the wall and said 'Is this the person you saw?' The grip said that it was, then kind of freaked out."

Marshall had once been a waiter at the legendary Brown Derby restaurant and was also the bar manager at the Legion Hall. The picture they have on the wall is of Marshall in a suit with a string tie looking just like a waiter.

The Highland Gardens Hotel

7047 Franklin Avenue, Hollywood, California 90028

Formerly known as the Hollywood Landmark hotel, The Highland Gardens Hotel was originally designed and built for entertainers, tourists, and Hollywood celebrities. The Hotel opened its doors in the mid 1950s utilizing classic Post and Beam architecture of the time. Because it is within walking distance to all major attractions and the studios, The Highland Gardens quickly became home to many famous Hollywood stars.

The Hotel has been used as a location site for television shows, fashion photography, and casting events, and past guests include members of the Rat Pack, Jefferson Airplane, Siegfried & Roy, and many more. It is also well known as the place where music icon Janis Joplin took her final bow in room 105 in 1970.

Joplin was an American blues-influenced rock singer and occasional songwriter with a distinctive, whisky tenor voice. She performed on four albums recorded between 1966 and 1970 — two as the lead singer of San Francisco's Big Brother and The Holding Company and two released as a solo artist. Joplin was posthumously inducted to the Rock and Roll Hall of Fame in 1995, and received a Grammy Lifetime Achievement Award in 2005.

She was ranked #41 on VH1's The 100 Greatest Artists of Rock 'n Roll in 1998, the third highest ranking for a female (only behind Aretha Franklin and Joni Mitchell) on the list. In 1999, she was ranked #3 on VH1's The 100 Greatest Women in Rock and Roll (effectively the same position). In 2004, *Rolling Stone* magazine ranked Joplin #46 on their list of the 100 Greatest Artists of All Time.

Cultivating a rebellious manner early on in her career, Joplin styled herself in part after her female blues heroines, and in part after the Beat poets. She left Texas for San Francisco in 1963, lived in North Beach, in Haight-Ashbury, and in Corte Madera. Around this time she acquired a reputation as a "speed freak" and occasional heroin user. She used other intoxicants as well. She was also a heavy drinker and her trademark beverage was Southern Comfort.

According to Hollywood historian Scott Michaels, Janis was in Los Angeles taping her final album, "Pearl," in October of 1970. On the evening of October 3rd, she and band member Ken Pearson were drinking screwdrivers at Barney's Beanery, a local hangout. Shortly after midnight, they drove back to the Hotel. Once inside her room, Janis shot up her last fix of heroin, then went down to the hotel lobby to get change for a five dollar bill for cigarettes. She chatted casually with the hotel clerk, who didn't know who she was, then returned to her room and collapsed beside the bed. She was found by John Cook, one of her band members, wedged bottoms up against a bedside table, with a cigarette in her hand.

Janis was cremated at Westwood Memorial Park on October 10th and her ashes were scattered over Stinson Beach, in Marin County. She had provided $1,500 dollars in her will for a funeral party, where The Grateful Dead performed for 200 of her friends.

The last recordings she completed were "Mercedes Benz" and a birthday greeting for John Lennon on October 1, 1970.

Lennon, whose birthday was October 9, later told talk show host Dick Cavett that her taped greeting arrived at his home after her death.

Her career had been meteoric, but her ascent as the first goddess of rock was doused by her sad, lonely death, which followed that of Jimi Hendrix, who'd died two weeks earlier. Jim Morrison would also be dead within a year.

When the television show *Dead Famous: Ghostly Encounters* went in search of the ghost of Janis Joplin, they didn't go to the Highland Gardens, but psychic Chris Fleming says that the show was one of his top three favorite episodes and, while it was edited out of the program, Chris did indeed have a visit with the rocker's ghost during filming.

"They did a hypnotic regression with me at Symphony Square, one of the locations we filmed at," said Chris. "At first I didn't think it was working, but then all of a sudden I slipped right into it and I crossed over to the astral plane and there was Janis Joplin. To me, it's probably one of the top five highlights of my entire life. What I saw, what she showed me, was beyond anything I ever expected."

Chris went on to say that he went into it with a list of questions in mind that he wanted to ask her, like how she felt about how she was treated when she was alive, what does she look like now, is she happy, and things like that. "Those questions were answered in just one second and I didn't even have to ask," he said. "It was just the experience itself, of what she showed me and what I felt. She held my hand, just looked at me and she goes, 'Did I answer all your questions?' and I said 'Yeah.'

"Because of what I experienced right there, I didn't want to come back, and it took them about a half hour to pull me out of it. I didn't want to leave. I wanted to stay right there and it got very emotional afterwards. The producers felt that nobody would believe it, and also that the experience didn't fit the "scary" aspect of the show because it was more warm and spiritual in nature, so they left it out of the broadcast, which was a shame."

Just a warning for anyone who goes to the Highland Gardens to look for Joplin's ghost. The owners of the hotel do not allow anyone other than paying guests to set foot in room 105. Media and lookie-loos are not welcome.

Celebrities Who Live in Haunted Houses

W e all think of celebrities as being larger than life with not a care in the world, but some of Tinseltown's biggest stars live with a problem that even the most efficient personal assistant can't handle. Ghosts. In Hollywood there is an abundance of infamous movie star ghosts who return to their old haunts on a regular basis, but there are also a great many non-celebrity spirits who haunt a group of famous folk who are very much alive. Here are the current batch of the most frequently told stories of celebrity ghost encounters.

Nicholas Cage

It has been reported that Nicolas Cage refused to sleep over at in his movie mogul uncle Francis Ford Coppola's home after he spotted a ghost in the attic. The Oscar-winning actor said he was terrified by the spooky sighting, which he initially mistook for a relative. It is reported that he was living in the attic at the time and there were bats living between the walls who would make scratching sounds all night. One evening, Cage was just dozing off when the door in front of the bed opened by itself to reveal a dark silhouette of a woman with big hair. The actor mistook the apparition for his aunt who he thought was coming to say goodnight, but when he said, "Goodnight," there was no response. Then the figure began to move towards him and when he realized it wasn't his flesh and blood relative, he froze up, let out a bloodcurdling scream, threw a pillow at it, and the apparition promptly disappeared.

Cage has been quoted as saying that he's not admitting that he actually saw a ghost, but whatever it was terrified him.

Neve Campbell

Neve Campbell, star of *Scream* and *The Craft* says that she lives in a haunted house and that living with a ghost adds to her paranoia about the paranormal. She once told an interviewer, "Someone was murdered in my house six years ago before I bought it. I had friends around and I left them in the living room to go in the kitchen and they both thought I had just walked back in again but I hadn't, so what they saw was the women who was murdered. The previous owner had a exorcist come in, but I don't think it worked."

Matthew McConaughey

Actor Matthew McConaughey claims to have freaked out the first time he saw the ghost of an old woman, whom he calls "Madame Blue," floating around his house. Feng-shui fan Matthew bought the 1969 three-bedroom house because "it has great lungs," but he quickly discovered the place was haunted. "When I first moved in there I had a tent and I put it up on the floor of the upstairs bedroom with my sleeping bag," he told reporters. "That's when I first saw Madame Blue. The first night I'm hearing noises, I'm hearing bass sounds, wood moving and coyotes, but then I hear this sound like a dime dropping from ten feet off the ground onto a glass table. I popped up out of the tent and went, 'That's too much trouble man, that's man made, and that was not the house.' So, I get up out of the tent with my dog and I'm running around buck naked and I've got a bat so I'm gonna go an investigate. I go downstairs and there's nothing there. I now know it was there because I have seen her since. She has no qualms with me —we get along just fine. She's a cool ghost. Maybe me being nude all the time is why we get along!"

Hugh Grant and Bette Davis

British actor Hugh Grant says he and friends have heard the wailing and screaming of some tormented spirit in his Los Angeles home. He even speculates it might be the ghost of a former resident, Bette Davis. The actress is said to haunt the Los Angeles apartment Grant owns in Los Angeles' Colonial Building. He and other residents have heard the tortured spook wailing and screaming in the night whenever tenants move into her old apartment.

Dan Aykroyd and Cass Elliot

Ghostbusters star Dan Aykroyd, who has always been fascinated with the paranormal, believes his home, once owned by Cass Elliot of The Mamas and The Papas, is haunted. "A ghost certainly haunts my house," he said. "It once even crawled into bed with me. The ghost also turns on the Stairmaster and moves jewelry across the dresser. I'm sure it's Mama Cass because you get the feeling it's a big ghost."

Billy Bob Thornton

Billy Bob Thornton's website claims that the actor lives above a haunted cave which he now uses as his music studio. The blurb on billybobthornton.net states: "Yes, it's haunted, and yes, it has secret passages that wind beneath Beverly Hills all the way to the border with West Hollywood. The Cave used to be a speakeasy during the Roaring '20s. Now, it's a cozy recording studio, built originally by Slash of Velvet Revolver when he, Mrs. Slash, and several snakes lived in the house (which was also owned by Cecil B. DeMille, among others). Now that the snakes are gone, it serves as Billy Bob's home away from home within his home. Sanctuary for Billy Bob's restless creativity, this recording studio has hosted some of rock, blues, pop, and country's finest talents, as well as that now-famous spirit."

Sting

Rock star Sting and his wife, Trudie, have also seen ghosts in their home. "I was absolutely terrified," he said. "I now believe those things are out there, but I have no explanation for them."

Jennifer Love Hewitt

We all know that actress Jennifer Love Hewitt talks to ghosts on her hit TV show, but she claims to have lived with one as well. *The Ghost Whisperer* star says she lived in a haunted house until a real-life *ghostbuster* came in and rid the place of not one, but two ghosts. Hewitt told her haunted tale during an interview on *The View*. She said that one of the ghosts was a woman who had known a previous owner of the house and the other was a young man who followed her home. The ghosts had been thumping around the house, turning on and off the lights, giving Hewitt the sniffles, and sapping her energy. The consultant came in, chatted with the ghosts who passed along messages to Hewitt, and then crossed over to their proper place in the afterlife, but Hewitt says she is not sure if they are actually gone or not.

Jean Claude Van Damme

Ghosts can even terrify movie tough guys like Jean Claude Van Damme, who still shivers at the image of a ghost he saw in his bathroom mirror. The Belgian actor continues to be wary of brushing his teeth in front of the mirror after his frightening experience. In explaining his ordeal the actor said, "I suddenly felt very cold. I turned round and thought, 'I've had a vision or something'. It was blue and white and had a very smoky body. Since that moment I've believed in ghosts."

Tim Robbins

Shawshank Redemption star Tim Robbins said a gaggle of ghosts caused him to move out of his Hollywood home in

1984. He had just moved into a new apartment in a converted church with his two cats. When he came home one night shortly after the move, it was quite dark and he could see that the cats were terrified. He felt as though there were spirits in the room. Then he looked on the wall and there were cockroaches all over it, so he moved out the next day.

Mick Jagger

In November 1990, Rolling Stone Mick Jagger was frightened off from buying a Gothic mansion by a bell ringing eighteenth century Ghost. Anna-Maria Sliwinski, the housekeeper of Donnington Grove House in Newbury, said of it, "I have heard the ghost firsthand. I heard strange chimes on a windless night. The bells were ringing in the tower, but there was nobody else in the house."

Ethan Hawke and Uma Thurman

Ethan Hawke and Uma Thurman were reportedly forced to flee from their plush eighteenth century home in Sneden's Landing, New York in 1998. The couple had only just bought the house in the star-studded hamlet when they discovered it was haunted. Local historians aren't surprised. They claim that all the houses in Sneden's Landing are haunted.

John Entwistle

The Who's bass guitarist John Entwistle, who passed away in 2002 was made a believer in the afterlife as the result of a supernatural encounter at his 188-year-old Gloucestershire, England, estate. He was convinced he had supernatural help from a ghost while he was creating the album for a now defunct TV show called *Van-Pires* and claimed that the benevolent spirit not only helped him with his musical career, it also kept unwelcome paparazzi away. Just shortly before his death, Entwistle said, "A lot of weird things have happened in the twenty-two years I've been here. Among them are sightings of a lady in nineteenth century clothes walking the grounds, and the camera of an uninvited photographer kept falling apart. Most recently I was having trouble locating a recording of Keith Moon pounding out a never-used Who song, and so I asked my friendly ghost for a helping hand. A few hours later when I was about to give up the search, the tapes spontaneously fell off a shelf behind me revealing the Moon recording which had been hidden behind them."

The Osbournes

The Osbournes, who are spooky enough in their own right, claimed to have a negative being in front of their old house (the one where their TV reality series was shot) who reportedly hung out inside the grounds by the gate. This ghost was supposedly a prankster who did all sorts of mischief, like turning the sprinklers on whenever tour buses passed by. There are those who have said that after watching Sharon Osbourne spitefully toss a whole ham into their noisy neighbor's yard to get them to shut up on *The Osbournes*, it seems more likely that it was she, and not a ghost, who might have been responsible for turning on the sprinklers.

Meg Ryan

The property on the right side of Meg Ryan's home reportedly has a ghost. He's a nasty entity who was killed in Chicago during the prohibition. The ghost then traveled to Vegas and wrecked havoc there, then migrated to Los Angeles, and is now Meg's next door neighbor. He is said to interfere with her by causing mechanical and electrical problems to her car.

Aaron Spelling

Aaron Spelling, who is now unfortunately a ghost himself, claimed to have a family of ghosts hanging out on his property. They were killed by Native American Indians and died in the Midwest on the prairie in a covered wagon. Why they moved to the Spelling estate is anyone's guess, but whenever Spelling played a certain type of music, they would come into his house and hang out in a corner of the living room.

Kate Winslet

A while back, actress Kate Winslet bought herself a secret hideaway on the secluded west coast of England but had no idea the property came with its own ghost. The house once belonged to a worker at nearby Camelot Castle Hotel, and some believe it is haunted by a previous owner who died about seventy years ago. The ghost has been seen by residents of the town walking from the house to the hotel, as if on his way to work. John Mappin, joint owner of the hotel, said that he hoped the ghost wouldn't put Kate off, because he's definitely friendly.

Renee Zellweger

Renee Zellweger called in a psychic when her new home in the Hamptons was found to contain a resident from the "other side." Renee was told that a ghost named Lillian had been living at the house for a number of years. A former owner of the house claimed that the ghost loved to play tricks. One night when he was lying in bed, he said it felt like there was a large block of ice next to him.

Tobey Maguire

It's said that friends of *Spider-Man* star Tobey Maguire have nicknamed him *Spooky Man* because of his fascination with things that go bump in the night. He regularly hosts séances at his Beverly Hills home, which he thinks is haunted. "There's definitely someone there with me," he says. "but it doesn't scare me. It's nice to have the company."

My haunted neighborhood.

The Ghost Stops Here

The homes on the quiet little street where I live were built in the early 1920s as housing for the employees of the nearby Hollywood Studios, Inc. which was built in 1919. After doing extensive research and having lived in this area for a very long time, I can't find any information which explains why many of the houses on this block are haunted — but they are. Three out of the first six houses on the block have quite a bit of paranormal activity associated with them.

I was eleven years old when my grandparents bought a house on this street, and I was happy to be moving here because the duplex where we lived had always scared me. My bedroom and the only bathroom were located at the back of the house, and the only way to get there was by going down a long, dark hallway.

My friend, Jenette, lived in the other side of the duplex with her grandparents, and because the living spaces were mirror images of each other, she also had to contend with a dreaded hallway. The wall between the two units was thin, so we could always tell which part of the house the other was in because we both navigated our hallways in an all-out, noisy run.

While Jenette never said much about her bedroom being scary, a lot of activity seemed to go on in mine. The closet door would frequently open and close by itself in the middle of the night, and I'd often wake up very early in the morning because my bed would be shaking so hard, I felt as though something was trying to toss me out. Needless to say, I was glad to be moving away from what I then referred to as the "spooky house of horrors."

When we first did a walk through of the new house, I didn't get the sense that anything was amiss. I think that was partially due to inattention because I was immediately drawn to the backyard which contained a small playhouse that I immediately claimed as my own.

After we moved in, I began to notice that certain areas of the house just didn't feel right. I could never walk into my grandparents' room, the master bedroom which was at the front of the house, without feeling the need to turn around and run back out. At first, I blamed the unsettling atmosphere on the dour, unsmiling portraits of my great grandmothers that hung on the south wall of the room. But when my other grandmother, Grandma Brooks, came to visit not long after we moved in, I took her into the room and she confirmed that something just wasn't right about it and suggested I say a prayer of protection whenever I had to go in there.

Because most of our neighbors were my grandparents' age and kept pretty much to themselves, I had no way of knowing whether or not there was any ghostly activity going on in their homes, but when a new family moved in down the street with a daughter who was my age, I came to realize that my house wasn't the only one with a creepy front bedroom.

My friend Ginny's room had the same eerie feeling to it as my grandparents' room did and she swore it was haunted. The knob to her bedroom door would rattle, turn, and then the door would fly open all by itself. One night Ginny awoke with the feeling that someone was watching her. She tried to talk herself out of it until that invisible "someone" sat down at the foot of her bed leaving a deep impression in the covers. When it happened again the next night, she got up and ran into her parents' room. Because her father worked the graveyard shift and wasn't home at the time, she jumped into bed with her mother. Her parents' room was just down the hall from hers and they had a clear view of Ginny's closed bedroom door. While she was trying to explain to her mother what had just happened, they looked down the hall just in time to see the doorknob turn and the door fly open on its own accord.

Out of the Frying Pan and Into the Fire

Back at my house, the strange activity began to escalate as well. One night I was alone at home and watching TV when a candle that was sitting on one of the end tables slid across the table and fell to the floor. Thinking that I must have set it too close to the edge, I picked it up and put it back on the middle of the table, only to have the same thing happen again a moment later.

Whenever I was alone in the house, I never really felt alone. I'd hear footsteps and loud bangs from time to time, and whenever Ginny or Jenette came over to spend the night, they both complained that the guest room gave them the creeps.

I moved out of the house and into my own apartment a couple of years after I graduated from high school but came back to the neighborhood several years later when the house next door to my grandparents' house came up for sale. By then Grandma was a quite elderly widow and I thought she'd appreciate me living next door, so I bought the house and moved back into the 'hood.

After my grandmother passed away, I rented out her house to an elderly woman, Mary, and her two grown sons. Mary took over my old bedroom and would often complain to me about the covers being flung off her in the middle of the night or pictures flying off the wall for no reason. Her sons slept in the front bedroom and regularly reported strangeness going on in there, too.

It wasn't very long after I moved into my new house next door that things began to happen here as well. I was in the kitchen one morning washing dishes when I saw the dark shape of a man with a pronounced limp walking down the driveway towards the garage. Thinking is must have been the meter man, I ran out the back door to check, but nobody was there, and because it was a fenced-in yard, there was no way anyone could have gotten out.

Knowing about the activity in the front bedrooms in my old house and Ginny's, I decided to sleep in the back bedroom and turn the front bedroom into a den. I was living alone at the time with three cats and a large black Lab. One evening I was in the den talking to Ginny on the phone when I saw the animals all staring at the same thing. It looked as though they were watching a tennis match with their heads moving in unison back and forth across the room. Suddenly the dog began to growl, the cats started hissing, and not wanting to stick around to see what was going to happen next, I told Ginny that I'd have to call her back and bolted out of the room.

Since then, that particular room has been a hotbed of activity, and I won't go in there alone after dark. When my boyfriend, Ken, moved in a few years ago, he turned the scary room into a "man's den" but soon found out that he wasn't always in there alone. On more than one occasion, he's seen the apparition of an old woman in a nightgown glide across the room and right through the wall to the living room. I've seen a large white mist go through the wall from the living room into the den. Both of us hear our names being called quite often when we're alone, things frequently go missing only to be found days later in the most unlikely places, and orbs frequently show up in photos and on night vision video.

One night Ken fell asleep in front of the television in there and woke up at two in the morning by what he described as a "light show." When he looked out into the hall, he saw a black shape pacing back and forth in front of the kitchen door. He's also been smacked in the head by unseen hands and hears someone wolf-whistling to get his attention.

The most recent occurrence happened not too long ago. I was standing at the stove making dinner when a medallion that I wear around my neck fell off the chain and landed at my feet. Thinking that the chain must have somehow opened up, I gave it a tug to pull it off but was startled to find that it was still firmly clasped around my neck. At that point, logic dictated that the jump ring on the medallion must have come open somehow, but when I bent down to pick it up and had a look, I was even more shocked to realize that the ring was one solid hoop so there was no way it could have opened up.

Because it seems as though the front part of many of the houses on this block are affected, I did some research on the area and couldn't come up with any tragedies that might have occurred. Native Americans lived in the area long before the houses were built, so this land might have been sacred to them; a place used in rituals perhaps, which would account for the great activity still happening in the area today.

A Little Help From My Friends

I was curious to find out who else was living in our house, so I invited psychic researchers Victoria Gross and Barry Conrad to come by and see if they could help solve the mystery of our haunted street.

As soon as they walked into the front bedroom, Barry said he felt lightheaded while Victoria became quite dizzy and neither felt at all comfortable in the room. Victoria then confirmed my suspicions that the northeast corner of the room was a portal, or gateway, where spirits enter our world from the other side.

Because some of the activity in the front bedroom was rather scary, I thought perhaps it might have something to do with an old World War II relic that I inherited when my mother passed away a few years ago, a Mauser pistol that my stepfather brought back from his tour of duty in Europe. Because the gun was a weapon of war, I wondered if the spirit of the gun's previous owner might have attached himself to it.

When I handed the gun to Victoria without telling her anything about it, she quickly put it down on the bed. "I'm not squeamish about firearms at all," she said, "but I don't like this one. It has killed quite a few people." Then she began having trouble with her throat.

"I feel like someone got shot in the throat," she said while repeatedly trying to clear her throat in order to get rid of the choking feeling. "There's a tall blond man attached to this weapon, and I get the impression that he eventually turned the gun on himself."

Since both the gun and the bedroom itself were affecting Victoria physically, we decided that it was a good time to move on.

In the back bedroom and bathroom area, she sensed the strong presence of an older woman who seems to be there all the time. This woman, she said, seems to have died from a head injury resulting from a fall or a stroke, but Victoria felt that she is a protective spirit and means no harm. Then we walked back into the living room where both she and Barry felt as though they were being watched, and Victoria described a tall, gray-haired man standing over in the corner. A few minutes later she said that she saw the elderly woman walk from my office straight through a closed door into the bedroom.

Later that evening I asked Victoria to check out the garage because it always felt creepy, and she determined that a spirit person was indeed living in there. Barry picked up on the name *Weston* or some other similar two-syllable surname that began with a *W*. It was then that I turned my flashlight to a nearby imprint in the cement which read: *Polly Wilson 1939*. Barry also picked up the impression of a man holding a rake arguing with a man wearing suspenders about money. He said that this was probably sometime in the 1920s.

We then decided to walk up and down the block to see if she could figure out why this neighborhood might have so much activity. Victoria stopped in front of a house three doors down to the west and described an elderly woman sitting in the front window. Little did she know that the original owner of the house had been an elderly woman who passed away in a chair near the front window several years ago. The poor woman's lifeless body sat in that chair for two days before anyone realized that she was actually dead.

When we finally got back to my house, I asked Victoria to keep going further up the block to the east although I knew from talking to the neighbors there that none of them had anything paranormal going on in their houses. As soon as she passed my driveway and was in front of the house next door, she said, "The atmosphere down this way is so much lighter and the farther I go, the lighter it gets." Then she turned and walked back towards my house and when she got to the property line she said, "Yep. The ghosts stop here."

By the end of our investigation, Victoria confirmed that my house was indeed haunted, not just by the male and female presence, but by many spirits. "It's funny," she said, "but the back of the house is ghost stuff and the front part of the house is portal stuff."

All I know is that there's never a dull moment around here as far as hauntings are concerned and next time Barry and Victoria come by, they suggested doing a séance, so maybe we can finally find out who these spirits actually are and why they're still hanging around.

The Ricardo Montalban Theater

1615 N. Vine Street
Hollywood, California 90028

T he historic Ricardo Montalban
Theater is located in the heart
of Hollywood, just half a block south of Hollywood
and Vine.

The venue formally opened as The Wilkes Vine Street Theater on January 9, 1927, with Dreiser's *The American Tragedy* and has been a landmark in the entertainment industry ever since.

It wasn't long after Howard Hughes became the new owner, a couple of years later, that he had it remodeled and changed its name to The Mirror Theatre, which showed motion pictures. The marquee at the time read: "All the best Talkies... and only 25 cents... kiddies 10 cents." During The Depression the theater changed owners and was renamed the Lux Radio Playhouse and by 1937 there was yet another a new name on the marquee: Studio Theatre — CBS Radio Playhouse — KNX-Vine Theatre.

In 1954, Huntington Hartford became the new owner. Hartford was heir to the Great Atlantic and Pacific Tea Company fortune. His grandfather, George Huntington Hartford, and his uncles, John Hartford and George L. Hartford, privately owned the A&P Supermarket chain, which at one point had 16,000 stores in the U. S. and was the largest retail empire in the world. When his uncles died they had no heirs, so he inherited their fortune. Hartford bought the building for $200,000 from Columbia Broadcasting and extensively remodeled and "modernized" the theater at an additional cost of $750,000. He streamlined the building from the facade, to the lobby and through the auditorium. The new design was created by famed "decorator to the stars" named Helen Conway, who gave it a "fashionable" look popular at the time.

In 1960, Josephine Baker headlined a musical production wearing $200,000 worth of the latest Paris creations. "The Best Man" by Gore Vidal, opened just prior to the 1960 Democratic National Convention.

Hartford ran the theater successfully for ten years and then in 1964 he sold the property to James Doolittle (owner of the Greek Theater in the Hollywood Hills) for $850,000. Cary Grant had tried to buy the building, but lost to Doolittle, and the theater was renamed the Doolittle Theater after its new owner. KTLA television did a live opening broadcast as 2,000 people lined Vine Street to see the stars arrive at the gala. The opening performance was Helen Hayes in "What Every Woman Knows."

Over the next couple of decades, the theater would run into disrepair and it remained empty for several years until it was bought in 2000 by the UCLA. performing arts group "Nosotros," an organization founded in 1970 by actor Ricardo Montalban "to help fulfill the goals of persons of Spanish-speaking origin in the motion picture and television industry." Nosotros means "us" in Spanish and it is the group's mission to improve the image of people of Spanish-speaking origin as they are portrayed on the screen, help their members seek employment opportunities in the entertainment industry, and to train them by offering theater workshops and theater productions they can be a part of. The founding board included members Desi Arnaz, Vicki Carr, and Anthony Quinn.

The Show Still Goes On

Because the theater has such a rich, star-studded history, I asked psychic Victoria Gross and cameraman/paranormal researcher Barry Conrad to come along with me and see if any ghosts might be waiting for us in the wings.

We were greeted by Margarita Cannon, the artistic director of the Montalban Theater, and we asked her if she or any other staff members had ever noticed any kind of paranormal activity. She told us that a security guard, as well as other employees who have stayed at the theater overnight always hear lots of noises of an unexplained origin, and that she herself has seen a ghost onstage on more than one occasion.

"He's a young man, probably in his 30s with blondish, curly hair and he wears a very colorful shirt," she told us. "He looks like he's from the 1970s and when I see him, it looks to me like he's performing. He seems to be aware that he's being seen, but then always runs off."

Margarita also said that she felt as though the theater had a lot of blocked energy. "I get the feeling of a block from going forward and it has felt that way for a number of years and I just can't get it out. It's a big obstacle, and success here is difficult. It takes double effort all the time to get anything accomplished. It's not negative exactly, but it's like Mercury is in retrograde forever. There's a resistance to change. Being from New Mexico I'm tuned into energy, and that energy here is very, very strong."

Victoria agreed and said she felt as though it was "like an invisible wall that you can't get through. It's like somebody doesn't want anything to change."

Margarita then went on to tell us about the flow of famous people who had performed on the stage over the years. "The theater is in the center of Hollywood so anybody who was anybody has been on this stage. In recent years we've had Alan Alda, Ben Vereen, Lily Tomlin, Jack Black, the cast of

Rent, and *Jesus Christ Superstar.* The theater used to be a road-house, so many New York productions came through here as well. All theaters have a muse," she went on to say, "and it's interesting what we actors channel through. We're all conduits for all types of energy."

Because it was so dark in the auditorium as we began our investigation, Barry asked that the house lights be turned on. The lights weren't bright, but helped quite a bit. Then Victoria went off to investigate the balcony where she felt a presence while Barry and I remained on the stage.

On her way upstairs, Victoria sensed quite a lot of turmoil on the stairs themselves and then felt the strong presence of a spirit man and woman sitting up in the balcony. She felt that the man was from the 1950s and more of a guardian who was looking after the place, and that the woman was from a different time but also a rather benevolent spirit. Margarita admitted that she feels spooked up in the balcony and avoids going up there alone whenever possible. "I can never go up into the balcony without getting the feeling that I'm going to fall out of there and land on the first floor," she said, "so I do avoid going up there."

I tried to take a couple of photos of the balcony while Victoria was up there, but my photos came out completely black, even with the flash. I did, however, manage to capture a couple of very bright orbs on the stage's backdrop, and one in the audience section as well.

Victoria and I then went upstairs to check out the dressing rooms. At first, the atmosphere up there was rather flat and we didn't pick up much of anything, but as soon as we walked into back dressing room on the second floor, Victoria's breathing became labored and she felt as though she had encountered a spirit who had a heart problem in life. She got the impression that it was a female energy from the 1940s.

"I can see her as a little girl with blonde hair and tap shoes and I get the sense of the Vaudeville era, but I feel as though she's coming back here as an adult with black hair," said Victoria. "I'm getting the name "Jolee" or something like that, but she's also telling me that her stage name was Janet Meyer or Meyers. She doesn't just stay confined to this dressing room either. She walks all around the theater because she loves this place."

Technical director David Meiselman, who runs the theater's reparatory company confirmed that the second floor dressing rooms are indeed haunted and said that it seems as though the spirits also do their best to rid the theater of people they don't like. He says, "...one night in the ladies' dressing room on the second floor, there was a vanity where nobody had sat for the last few days. One of the actors came in and was standing in front of it when it just collapsed and fell on him. And then all of a sudden the lights went out. No one touched or bumped the vanity beforehand, but that's the dressing room where we have a lot of 'problems.' That's the one where all the stuff happens."

"Not long ago," said David, "the theater had been locked down for the night but 'somebody' unlocked the roof door. Nobody had been on the roof, but the door was somehow unlocked. Now I'm a big guy and not afraid of anything, but I wouldn't go up there, so I left the alarm off for the night and took care of it the next day instead."

He also says that periodically all the power suddenly goes out on the top floor. "It's like all the bulbs have been unscrewed and they turn off all at once. Also doors slam quite a bit and we hear all sorts of strange noises. It's pretty creepy sometimes."

And, according to David, not all the Montalban ghosts are friendly. "In the upstairs men's bathroom, there's a very heavy, dark masculine presence that many people have felt. He also moves through the theater. That's the presence that makes me not want to go up to the tower and probably the same presence that threw the vanity down. I've caught glimpses of this man in that dressing room and so have other people. He seems to be about six feet tall and is wearing a suit, but I've only seen him from behind, so can't give you a better description. He does really bad things in this place from time to time and my gut feeling is that something really bad went down in that men's room years ago."

When Victoria and I continued up to the third floor, she immediately felt quite dizzy in the hallway. "There's a strong male energy up here and I get the impression that he accosted a female. It's not an active haunting, but more like residual energy, but it's a creepy feeling nonetheless." Strangely enough, I took a photo of Victoria in that hallway, and when I looked at the picture in the camera's viewfinder, it looked as though the word "RUN!" appeared on the wall. When I came home and uploaded the photo to my computer, the image had disappeared.

Down in the basement green room, Victoria sensed quite a bit of energy and lots of activity. She sensed a mischievous spirit who seemed to be following us throughout the theater, but she said he was one step ahead of us all during our investigation, never staying still long enough for her to communicate with him. She thought he might be the same spirit that Margarita had seen running across the stage and described him as "a mischievous guy who just wants to play."

It's David's theory that the basement is relatively ghost-free and says he feels very safe in the catacombs down there and jokingly remarked, "I honestly feel that ghosts don't go down in places like that because they're scary." He also feels that the Montalban Theater ghosts know that the people working there have good intentions so they don't go out of their way to do bad things, although both David and Margarita agree that people who are not good for the theater don't last very long.

When I asked Margarita whether or not she would be comfortable spending the night at the theater alone her comment was, "Others have stayed here overnight, with no problem, except for hearing things, but no, I don't think I could. Sometimes when I come in early and open the theater by myself and it's very dark, I do feel uncomfortable."

Margarita said that in spite of all the unearthly goings on in his theater, Ricardo Montalban feels "very comfortable here," and she also said that most of the people who work there go about their business and work in harmony with the restless spirits. "This stage has been a fertile ground for so much talent, so many realized dreams and failed dreams, and as actors, we are conduits to so many spirits," she said, "but I think whatever is here is friendly, and I hope the spirits have found a home here and want to stay. They're good company and I do welcome them."

The Playful Ghosts of Yamashiro Restaurant

1999 N. Sycamore Avenue, Hollywood, California 90068

In Japanese, Yamashiro means "Mountain Palace," and for the past eighty-eight years the Yamashiro Restaurant has been perched high on a Hollywood hill majestically looking down at the city below. Originally built in 1911 by the Bernheimer brothers as a private home and a place where they could house their priceless collection of Asian treasures, the brothers brought in hundreds of skilled craftsmen from the Orient to recreate an exact replica of a palace located in the Yamashiro mountains near Kyoto, Japan.

The home took three years to build and when completed, 300 steps led up the hillside through superbly landscaped Japanese gardens to the ten-room teak and cedar mansion, where carved rafters were lacquered in gold and tipped with bronze dragons.

There is a Sacred Inner Court which forms a lovely garden in the center of the building and it is filled with plants, stone hewn pools, and some very large Koi fish. The Inner Court was built to provide light and air to the surrounding rooms whose walls were covered with lustrous silks and hung with antique tapestries. Although most customers who sit in this outdoor area and have dinner don't know it, the garden is also where the ashes of two former owners are buried.

The hillside terraces were filled with 30,000 varieties of trees and shrubs, waterfalls, hundreds of goldfish, and even a private zoo of exotic birds and monkeys. Miniature bronze houseboats floated along a maze of tiny canals through a miniature Japanese village.

Today, the oldest building in Los Angeles is Yamashiro's 600-900 year old pagoda which was brought from Japan and set beside a lake which once was home to rare black Australian swans. Unfortunately, most of the Asian collection, the Buddhist and Satsuma art, the rare jades, tapestries, and cloisonné chandeliers, were auctioned off in 1922 after one of the Bernheimer brothers died.

In the late 1920s Yamashiro served as headquarters for the ultra-exclusive "400 Club." Created for Hollywood's elite during its Golden Age, Yamashiro gave Hollywood its first celebrity hangout. A Who's Who of actors, writers, directors, and celebrities could be found there on any given night. During Prohibition, the expansive basement was used as a speakeasy, complete with a one-lane bowling alley and bar.

During World War II, the building was boarded up and the Japanese façade completely obstructed for fear someone would blow the place up due to the anti-Japanese sentiment of the time, but after the war ended, the building was completely restored, and before it became a restaurant in the 1970s, Yamashiro was used both as a boy's military academy and also as an apartment complex. It is rumored that the late Richard Pryor and actor Pernell Roberts both lived at Yamashiro.

Over the years, the restaurant has been used as a location for many movies. *Teahouse of the August Moon* was shot there, as was the Marlon Brando film *Sayonara*. In fact, one of the old rickshaws used in the movie is stored down in the basement, complete with a California driver's license attached to the back.

Yamashiro's 900-year-old pagoda.

Yamashiro's Resident Spirits

With such a long, rich history, I surmised that the building should be haunted, and after talking to Executive Assistant and Marketing Manager Carrie Farber on the phone, I was convinced that we would find a spirit or two. I invited psychic Victoria Gross and paranormal researcher Barry Conrad to come and investigate who Yamashiro's restless spirits might be.

Shortly after we arrived, Service Manager Nori Jill Philips said, "Everybody who works at the restaurant knows that Yamashiro is haunted, but not everybody talks about it. We have all had some type of experience. Whether people believe it or not, things happen here. Frequently. Lights go off and on by themselves, phones ring after they've been turned off, real-looking people can be seen walking past upstairs windows, the ghost of a former bartender still comes into work each night and sorrowful crying is frequently heard in the Bride's Room.

When Victoria went upstairs to the Bride's Room to investigate, she said that the atmosphere felt very dense and she got the impression that the crying was that of a child, probably dating back from the time when the building was a private home. She didn't think it was an active haunting or the result of a trapped spirit, but of residual energy.

This was also where Victoria picked up the presence of an aggressive male figure standing at the window looking down at the patio. She believes him to be from the time when the building was used as a boy's military academy. She also felt a "weird sadness" to the room and said it had a whole different vibe than the rest of the place. We were told that this was one of the areas that many employees try and avoid, if possible. The other area is the basement.

Carrie Farber has heard ghost stories about the restaurant from the first day she began working there and although she's never had an experience herself, she agrees that the basement is one of the scariest places in the whole restaurant. "Most employees will not go down there alone," she says, "because they've seen and heard too many unsettling things down there."

Ex-employee Tommy Zoobharasee, who managed the restaurant for ten years, agrees. "One evening, I was sitting with some friends out on the patio and was telling them about all the ghostly encounters I've had here at Yamashiro and they didn't believe me. A while later, I gave them a tour of the restaurant, then took them down to the basement. We went down into the liquor room and then passed the maintenance bathroom and saw nothing, but once we reached the door to come back upstairs, the bathroom door suddenly slammed shut by itself. It sounded so loud that all of us turned around. There was no way the door could have slammed by itself because there are no windows or drafts down there. At that moment, we all decided it was time to leave and rushed up the stairs. That experience made believers out of my friends."

During Prohibition, parts of the basement were used as a Speakeasy and there is one narrow room that had once housed one-lane bowling and a bar. As we were investigating that room, we suddenly heard the sound of loud moaning. We all heard it and Carrie then admitted that when she was opening up the door to let us in, she heard it then, too. "I didn't say anything at the time," she said, "but I was kind of afraid to open the door because it was so loud, I was worried that we were going to find a couple of the employees back in there making love."

To see if I could actually capture any other ghostly sounds, I turned on my digital voice recorder but didn't pick up anything else. Victoria did make contact with the spirit of a man who seemed to be from the 1920s and was confined to the area. She also saw a bright flashing light at one end of the room. Just as we were leaving the area, I saw what can only be described as a streak of light whizzing past the back of Barry's head.

The hauntings are both visual and auditory and they eventually make believers out of the most ardent skeptics. Tommy Zoobharasee has had his share of ghost sightings even though he did not believe in ghosts when he first started working at the restaurant.

"My first experience with a ghost was when I went up to the employee's locker room. I was the only one up there, and as soon as I walked in the door, a crumpled paper towel hit me on my back. I turned around and saw it laying on the floor beside me and I knew nobody else was there, but at the time I still didn't believe in ghosts.

"Then one evening I was sitting alone in the bar after closing. Everyone else had gone home and suddenly the phone began to ring. When I picked it up, nobody was there and I didn't think much about it. But then this happened three times in a row and the phone rang twice each time meaning that the call was coming from a location in-house. When it happened the third time, I finally looked down at the phone to see what part of the restaurant the call was coming from and the display said that the call originated from bar where I was sitting!"

The bar is also the place where the ghost former bartender hangs out, and Tommy was the first to see him.

"I was sitting with my ex-wife and a group of friends after closing one night when out of the corner of my eye, I saw someone wearing a white t-shirt walking from the dining room into the bar, but when I looked into the bar to see who it was, there was nobody there. My ex-wife looked towards the bar and I saw her eyes get really big and she jumped up and flew into the lap of a guy who was sitting across the table. She'd seen him, too.

The description Tommy and his ex-wife gave of the apparition fit the description of a man named Norman who had worked at the bar for thirty-five years. And that was the incident that finally made him believe in ghosts.

During our walk around, Victoria encountered a mournful female spirit sitting alone in the southwest corner of the restaurant at Table 8. According to the staff, that is the most popular table in the restaurant. The entity was quite somber and was sitting there looking out the window at the spectacular view of the city.

"She's alone now," said Victoria, "but she wasn't lonely when she was alive. I think she's sitting here waiting for somebody she used to come here with to pass over to the spirit world, but the thing is, he's already passed over and she doesn't know it. I think it was her husband, and this is where she chooses to wait for him. She's so focused on her plight, she is blocking out everything else and isn't even aware that we're here, so any communication I could be having with her is completely blocked. It's like I'm the one that's in the spirit world to her."

Sadly, without being able to communicate with this poor soul who Victoria named Margaret as a point of reference, there was no way to let the her know that if she only crossed over to the other side, her husband would be there waiting for her.

The kitchen also seems to have an afterlife of it's own and people who work in there quite often complain of dizziness and having the hair stand up on the back of their necks.

Out on the patio, Victoria picked up a male spirit looking down out of a second floor window, which now contains the restaurant's business offices and the locker room for employees. Nori Phillips says that when people use the bathroom in the locker room, the minute they shut the bathroom door, they hear the lockers being opened and closed in the adjoining room even though nobody else is there.

Victor Torres, the restaurant's head cook for the past ten years can also attest to the fact that the locker room is indeed haunted.

Table 8 where the lonely lady spirit sits.

"One night I took a break around 11:30 and went upstairs. I sat down and all of a sudden, one of the windows, which was about five feet away from me began to open and close on its own. That window is always closed because it's so hard to open."

Victor is not the only one to experience this phenomenon. While we were there conducting our investigation, an employee who had only been working at the restaurant for the past week came over to inform us that while he was up in the employee rest room just a few minutes before, a small window blew open on its own and when he went over to lock it back up, he noticed that it was not an easy lock to latch and said that he had to apply a great deal of pressure to close it and couldn't understand how it could possibly have opened up on its own.

Victor frequently gets the feeling that someone is following him around or brushing past him, but when he turns around, there's never anybody there. Who that spirit might be is an unknown, but one thing Victor knows for sure is that the Yamashiro ghosts don't like loud people. He says that if someone gets too rambunctious, the spirits will warn them to quiet down by flicking the lights off and on.

Another of the restaurant's former bartenders always used to feel someone patting him on the back while he was working behind the bar. Maybe Norman, who seems to keep a watchful eye on the bar, was just letting the guy know that he was doing a fine job.

The ghostly activity is not just confined to the main building. Looking down at the ancient pagoda on the beautifully landscaped grounds, Victoria picked up on lots of energy, much more energy than in the main building itself. "The property just feels really blessed," she said. "You can just see the ancient ones around the pagoda and they are its guardians. They came along with it from Japan when the building was brought here. You can feel them here on the walkway which leads down to it."

"Yamashiro has such a rich and amazing history," said Carrie Farber, "and nobody has ever had a bad encounter with any of our ghosts. They are seen and heard everywhere, but they're more playful than scary, and I think they are just here to protect us."

Boardner's Bar

1652 N. Cherokee Avenue, Hollywood, California 90028

A local hangout for the "Who's Who & Who Cares," Boardner's has been one of Hollywood's best kept secrets since 1942.

Visiting Boardner's is like taking a step back in time and the ghosts of its storied past are evident the minute you walk through the door. With its black leather booths and dim lighting, the atmosphere is very reminiscent of the 1940s and a sense of Old Hollywood is definitely in the air.

Back in its heyday, former Tommy Dorsey singer Jack Leonard would regularly drop in, as would Errol Flynn, and members of Xavier Cugat's band. Another regular patron was singer and bandleader Phil Harris whose routine was to say goodbye to his wife, Alice Faye, after the two dined at Musso & Frank, then head over to Boardner's for a rendezvous with his mistress. George Gobel, Pat O'Brien, Nick Adams, Lucille Ball, and many others wined and dined at the tavern after a hard day's work.

One day in 1946, regulars W. C. Fields and Wallace Beery were seated in a booth and ordered Coca-Colas. "Coke?" owner Steve Boardner joked. "Why, that stuff'll kill you." Ironically, within the year, Fields was dead from cirrhosis of the liver complications.

Death came to another customer, Elizabeth Short, later known as the Black Dahlia, about a year later. "She'd always have two or three sailors hanging off her arm," said Boardner in an interview a few years ago. "She'd come over here from Bradley's Five & Ten, which sold short beers for a nickel, longs for a dime and shots of bourbon for fifteen cents." Contrary to local urban legend, however, Boardner's was not Short's last call before immortality.

Long after Hollywood's nightlife began its decline with the end of World War II, the tavern continued to be a meeting place for entertainers. Legend has it that one day in 1956, Johnny Carson came in and wanted to tend bar. The bartender used to flip empty Lucky beer bottles up in the air by the neck and toss them in the case they came in. When Johnny tried it, the bottle hit him right in the eye.

Director Ed Wood was a Boardner's regular, as was Alan Hale Jr., Mickey Mantle, and Joe DiMaggio.

Over time, the bar, like Hollywood itself, began to lose its luster. In the late 1950s and early '60s, KNX entertainment broadcaster Tom Hatten was an actor appearing in The Billy Barnes Revues at the nearby Las Palmas Theater, and he'd go over to Boardner's with his friends after rehearsals. He told an interviewer a few years ago that he remembers the bar as "kind of dank and tacky, but fun. Most of us didn't have much money, and Boardner's had good steak sandwiches."

In recent years, Boardner's has taken on a new life, but remnants of the past still remain. Tricia LaBelle, who has owned the bar since 1998, claims that Boardner's is haunted by more than just memories. "Some of my staff have experienced music going on and off, TVs on and off and flipping channels, and we actually have a picture taken by a customer with two apparitions in the window behind them, a man in a top hat and a woman in a black veil. We've seen spirits standing on the staircase in the club and heard someone walking on the staircase leading up to the office. There have been two deaths here as well. One was a previous owner who slumped over dead at the bar on Christmas Eve 1997, and the other was a little old man who used to live upstairs in the office on a day bed. A ghost has been seen in the tiny women's room upstairs in the office as well. Many of our employees don't want to be here alone, if they can help it."

Employee Lynn Dougherty agrees that she'd rather not be in the building by herself and said that she was pretty apprehensive when she first started working there. "I heard stories from the old manger who would see people who weren't there and would sometimes feel something brush up against her, but now I'm used to it," said Lynn, "so these things don't really bug me anymore. When I come in by myself, I just call out, 'Okay, I'm here, just settle down' and get on with my work."

Jeffrey, Jonathan, and the Dark Phantom

With such a rich Hollywood history and great ghost stories, paranormal researcher Barry Conrad and psychic medium Victoria Gross came with me to check out the Boardner's ghosts, and we weren't disappointed.

As soon as we walked through the front door, Victoria sensed quite a bit of activity. "This place is full of spirits and there's quite a bit of energy here. The minute I came in, it hit me," she recalls. "Right at the bar, I picked up the spirit of an older man who I'm going to call Jeffrey. He was just checking us out and I could hear him laughing. I got the impression that he's a jokester and I just wanted to laugh with him. There is also a lot of residual energy around from many powerful people, of deals being made, contracts being negotiated, lots of laughter, and just a good overall feel to the place. It's quite jovial."

Outside on the patio, Victoria got a strong sense of the 1940s and said the atmosphere surrounding her felt very genteel in one particular area over by the small open air stage. "I picked up the layers of the spirits there and then the energy of the place. I saw beautiful women of the 40s dressed in the Hollywood style of the day. It was all very glamorous, but at the same time it was like the extreme past was being pushed away by a newer, stronger energy and it was so intense and drastic compared to the elegant feeling of the 40s. It's a whole new generation that these older spirits don't understand."

That change in atmosphere could possibly be because on weekends, Boardner's transforms itself into Bar Sinister, a Goth bar.

Victoria was then drawn to the stage where she got the strong impression that one spirit in particular was extremely distressed by the bar's current customers.

"He was a very angry man," she said, "and I got the feeling that he was a want-to-be actor who was very good at his craft, but wasn't very successful and didn't get the break he deserved. He gave me the name Jonathan, and I saw him as tall, kind of slender, with very fair skin and dark hair; much younger than the spirit I felt inside at the bar."

"Jonathan seems to be frustrated that he can't be seen. He wants people to watch him and is pacing back and forth because he doesn't want to be ignored." Because he was a troubled soul and not at peace, Victoria was able, with Jonathan's consent, to call upon the angelic forces to come and assist him in crossing over.

In the long alleyway just off the patio, Victoria picked up lots of negative energy and quickly determined that two murders had taken place in the area; the strangulation of a woman, probably sometime in the 1940s, and the knifing of a man several years later. She also felt the presence of a dark figure crouching behind a dumpster at the far end of the alley. Victoria referred to him not as a ghost, but as a lower entity that she calls a phantom.

"He's a feeder and feeds off the energy trapped in the alley as well as that of people who walk past here," she said. "He's what we call a 'bottom feeder' and I feel very uncomfortable around him." (Victoria advises that a *bottom feeder* is a made-up term referring to someone who is of a lower class of person, oftentimes criminally minded, a dreg of society. A *phantom* is just another term for ghost, although some people will classify them as coming from a lower realm without human origin.)

Lynn then took Victoria upstairs in the office, where the atmosphere was uncomfortable in another way. "It feels as though my life energy is being sucked out of me. I'm overtaken by a strong sense of fatigue and feel so depleted. It feels like someone just sucker-punched me," she said. "It's also quite hard to breathe, and my throat suddenly got very sore."

According to Lynn, the previous owners had been heavy smokers.

While they were upstairs in the office where much of the paranormal activity is centered, both Victoria and Lynn heard scratching noises that they could not find a reasonable cause for in spite of rooting around looking for mice. Obviously, someone was trying to get their attention.

Tricia, Lynn, and the other employees of Boardner's Bar have learned to take the hauntings in stride. "It's all kind of exciting, and I think the ghosts are here to protect us," says Tricia. "After all, we're here in Hollywood and weird stuff happens!"

The Hollywood Heritage Museum

2100 N. Highland Avenue, Hollywood, California 90068

This famous old barn is situated on a patch of green lawn right across the street from the Hollywood Bowl. Built in 1896, the sign above its porch simply reads "*Lasky-DeMille Barn*" and gives no apparent clue that this unassuming building is one of the most historic structures from the Golden Age of Hollywood. In fact, Cecil B. DeMille's tombstone at nearby Hollywood Forever Cemetery is much more impressive.

The DeMille Barn was the very first major movie studio in Hollywood.

In 1913, director DeMille rented the former horse barn for $250 a month, and used it to shoot Hollywood's first full-length feature film, *The Squaw Man*. The actors used the empty stalls as dressing rooms, and while DeMille was shooting the film, the barn's owner actually kept his horse and carriage inside the "studio."

The Squaw Man, in which DeMille appeared as an extra, went on to become a major box-office smash. It was the first hit movie made in Los Angeles. The film cost $15,000 to make and grossed over $200,000 nationwide. This led to Hollywood becoming the movie capital of the world and the little "*Famous Players-Lasky Co.*" went on to become the giant Paramount Studios.

Cecil DeMille's grave at Hollywood Forever Cemetery.

The small barn/studio was originally located at 1521 Vine Street, just one block north of Sunset. Today, there is a plaque on the northeast corner pointing out the historic site. The studio/barn was moved to the nearby Paramount Studios lot in the 1920s where it spent the next fifty-five years being used in many productions, including being part of the *Bonanza* set.

In October 1979, Paramount gave the DeMille barn studio to Hollywood Heritage Inc. who then rescued it from demolition in 1982. The barn was moved to its current, permanent site by Hollywood Heritage and then beautifully restored. It is now open to the public as the *Hollywood Heritage Museum*.

In a strange twist of fate, I happened to be there the evening the barn was ceremoniously driven off to its new location. At the time, I had no indication of just how important the old building was, even though TV cameras and news crews from around the world were there to document the historic moment. I was just enthralled watching the trailer haul the old building out of the parking lot and slowly drive down the street with its precious cargo.

The Museum now houses the largest public display of early Hollywood photographs and memorabilia. Rare photos show significant silent film sets and casts, as well as views of Hollywood homes and the fantasy architecture that made Hollywood's boulevards unique. Charlie Chaplin's 1919 movie camera can be seen, along with 1929 movie projectors used by Buster Keaton in his home.

There is a large assortment of actual props and weapons from DeMille films (spears, shields, swords, etc.), including *The Ten Commandments, The Crusades, Cleopatra* and *Samson and Delilah*.

One corner of the barn contains Cecil B. DeMille's private office, complete with his original desk, telephone, and typewriter. You can also see DeMille's glasses, shoes, riding gloves, and crop on display. Visitors are invited to watch a forty-five-minute video on De Mille and his most famous movies.

It's been said that that all objects have the potential for housing spirit energy and some spirits have a lingering fondness for certain of their most cherished possessions. It's not unusual for them to come back every so often to keep an eye on them. In short, any object that was important to or cherished by someone in life can be watched over by that someone's ghost. With that in mind, one can't help but wonder whether or not Mr. DeMille stops by the barn from time to time to perhaps sit behind his old desk, watch one of his old movies, or use the telephone to make an ethereal phone call or two. Or perhaps Charlie Chaplin or Buster Keaton pop in to make sure their cherished equipment is being kept in good order.

In September 1996, the DeMille barn suffered a disastrous fire, which almost gutted the old studio. The fire charred the back and roof of the building, while smoke and water damaged several pieces of historic movie memorabilia. They lost the litter from *The Ten Commandments* and the chariot from the 1926 *Ben-Hur,* but fortunately the structure itself survived, and the firemen were able to rescue many of the museum's other valuable artifacts.

The museum has been painstakingly restored in the years since the fire, and on July 10, 1999, the staff of Hollywood Heritage reopened the Museum to the public.

Dining with The Dead

The Janes House — 6541 Hollywood Boulevard

The Janes House is a beautiful two-story Queen Anne/ Dutch Colonial Revival home with shingled gables and fanciful turrets on busy Hollywood Boulevard, just a few blocks east of the Chinese Theater. The home was built back in 1903, when similar Victorian homes lined the boulevard (which was then called Prospect Avenue) and it is the only original Victorian mansion left standing on bustling Hollywood Boulevard.

Beginning in 1911, Janes House was a family-run school called The Misses Janes School of Hollywood, and its broad front yard was filled with the children of film industry VIP's. Mary Ruth Janes and her three daughters ran the well-respected school which offered education from kindergarten through eighth grade. Classes were often taught in the home's shady back yard. The school attracted the children of early Hollywood celebrities such as Charlie Chaplin, Douglas Fairbanks, Cecil B. DeMille, Noah Beery, Jesse Lasky, and the Chandler Family (who own the *Los Angeles Times*).

In 1926, hard times fell on the Janes sisters and they were forced to close their school. As Hollywood Boulevard grew around the charming little home, the sisters were forced to rent out their large front yard as a parking lot and to lease space there to a flower vendor. The home eventually fell into disrepair, along with the rest of old Hollywood Boulevard. The last of the Janes sisters, Carrie Belle, died in 1982.

Fortunately, through the efforts of Guy Miller, a young man whom the sisters had taken in during the 1970s, their home was saved and restored to its former glory.

Today, the cottage is stuck in the back of a modest, modern mini-mall called Janes Square. The gray and white shopping center is designed to imitate the shingled Victorian look of the Janes House itself. The center's retail spaces house a mix of electronic stores, gift shops, and the like.

In 2006, following an earlier renovation of the courtyard, the 102-year-old Janes House reopened as a restaurant named Memphis. It's a Southern/Cajun restaurant, but they kept the glitzy Victorian interior, complete with red silk and chandeliers. There's a bar and lounge on the ground floor, and the dining room is upstairs. It's a great place to see Hollywood celebrities as well.

According to staff members, the Janes House is definitely haunted. Doors and windows open and close by themselves and things move around all on their own. More than likely, the Janes sisters are just trying to let the new tenants know that they are still around.

El Compadre Restaurant — 7408 W. Sunset Boulevard

While none of the people who work at this Mexican restaurant owned up to having any resident ghosts, the El Compadre seems to have more than one lively spirit. Two of them reportedly walk near the piano after closing and are reported to be the ghosts of two ex-employees who were killed during a robbery back in the 1950s when the restaurant was known as Don Pepe. There is also another ghost that lurks by the mirror in the bar area.

Sweet Lady Jane — 8360 Melrose Avenue

Sweet Lady Jane is a world-famous gourmet bakery in West Hollywood very close to the reportedly haunted Cedars-Sinai Medical Center. Lady Jane's offers the most tempting of treats and, every once in a while, also gives unsuspecting customers a first hand glimpse (and whiff) of old Hollywood in the guise of the late actor/director Orson Welles.

Although the bakery opened in 1988 and Welles died in 1985, the location used to be the site of the old Ma Maison restaurant where Welles frequently dined. Employees and customers have reported smelling cigar smoke near the area of Welles' old table, and his distinctive apparition, wearing a black cape, has also been seen sitting at the table taking it all in. Could it be that the delicious aroma of Lady Jane's heavenly desserts draws the actor back to his old haunt, or is it simply residual energy replaying happy times that people report seeing? After all, the rotund actor did love his food.

Gloria Pink, owner of the world-famous Pink's Hot Dog Stand, which has been at the same location at Melrose and La Brea since 1939, said Pink's was one of Welles' favorite hangouts. He is said to have once eaten 18 hot dogs in one sitting!

Musso and Frank's Grill-6667 Hollywood Boulevard

In operation since 1919, Musso and Frank's is Hollywood's oldest and most enduring restaurant. Originally owned by John Musso and Frank Toulet, it was, and still is, a restaurant frequented by many celebrities. When I went there for a business lunch a couple of years ago, the restaurant was teeming with (living) members of the "Old Hollywood" establishment.

Back in 30s and 40s, rival gossip columnists Hedda Hopper and Louella Parsons frequently interviewed people at the restaurant for their newspaper columns. Charlie Chaplin, who liked their dry martinis, was also a regular, His favorite table was the first one when walking in the old room from Hollywood Boulevard, while silent-movie star Tom Mix preferred to dine next to the window so his fans could see him.

Humphrey Bogart, Jack Webb, and Peter Lawford were also frequent guests at the restaurant, and during Hollywood's Golden Years, Irving Thalberg, Clark Gable, and the Marx Brothers were among its most celebrated clients. These days, it's the likes of Henry Winkler, The Rolling Stones, Brad Pitt, Nicholas Cage, and Ben Kingsley who blend in well with the restaurant's oak-beamed ceilings, red-leather booths, mahogany room dividers, and chandeliers with tiny shades. Tom Selleck likes to sit at table 24 to enjoy offerings from the extensive old-school menu which is a veritable survey of American/Continental cookery. Actor Al Pacino reportedly prefers table 28.

While the restaurant belonged to the stars in the 1930s and 40s, its bar belonged to the screenwriters, whose guild was just across the street on Cherokee Avenue. After a hard day of working on the latest novel or screenplay, the bar was filled with America's finest literary luminaries, like William Faulkner, Ernest Hemingway, and F. Scott Fitzgerald, who probably wandered over from his digs at the Gardens of Allah on the nearby Sunset Strip. Faulkner, who lived in a nearby hotel, was such an authority on the Mint Julep that the bartenders at Musso's always let him mix his own.

The writers also claimed the "back room" where they would drown their sorrows. Aldous Huxley, Raymond Chandler, and Nathaniel West supposedly played poker back there. The famous back room soon came to be known as "the Algonquin of the West." It had been leased from the Vogue Theater in May of 1935, and was apparently lost around 1954, when they lost their lease. A long time maitre d' for the back room was Daniel Ilich, who so jealously guarded the space for the writers that he was fired when the owner discovered the room empty of regular customers, even though there was a long line waiting to be seated. The writers apparently were late in arriving because they'd been at the races. The back room still exists, but it has been closed to the public since the 1950s.

According to writer and former *Los Angeles Magazine* editor Joshua Tompkins, when he and renowned psychic Kenny Kingston had dinner together at Musso's a couple of years ago, the restaurant was filled with the ghosts of some of Hollywood's greatest stars.

"When we first arrived, things were pretty quiet, but just as I started to think that maybe the evening would be a flop as far as celebrity ghost sightings were concerned, Kenny's eyes fixed on something over my shoulder and he looked rather amused. I turned to see a young man, sitting a few tables away, scratching the back of his neck and then his nose. Kenny explained that the man was reacting like that because Errol Flynn was standing behind him, tickling him with a feather.

"Subsequently, Kenny went on to point out that the ghost of Lionel Barrymore was hovering around a group of four men sitting at a nearby table, and noticed that Orson Wells and Charles Laughton were, appropriately enough, bellying up to the bar. He said Carole Lombard was dueling with a live woman for control of a bar stool and later on he mentioned that Peter Lorre was over on the other side of the room, as was Jean Harlow." He also made mention of the fact that Raymond Burr seems to linger near the restrooms with a thin man that Kingston didn't recognize.

When Joshua asked if these famous souls appear every night, Kenny explained that on this particular evening, they were out in force because they knew Joshua was there to write about them, and then went on to explain that they love publicity now as much as they did on the Earth plane.

So if you're planning to visit Musso's the next time you're in Hollywood, remember that seeing the ghost of a dearly departed movie star may not be possible without the help of a psychic to point them out, but if you should decide to dine at the restaurant anyway and suddenly start feeling a bit itchy, don't blame it on Musso's famous Flannel Cakes. Just turn around and politely ask Errol Flynn to knock it off!

Kate Mantalini — 9101 Wilshire Blvd

Located on busy Wilshire Boulevard and named after a famous female boxing promoter of the 1940s, Kate Mantalini has been a local celebrity hangout since it opened in 1987. Recently it's becoming well known as the haunting grounds for Althea Flynt, former wife of Larry Flynt of *Hustler* magazine fame whose offices were upstairs in the same building. Althea drowned in the bathtub of the couple's Bel Air Mansion in 1987, but her ghost is said to haunt the restaurant.

Moonshadows — 20356 Pacific Coast Highway in Malibu

Moonshadows has been a popular hangout for celebrities and regular folk alike since it opened in 1971. Back in the 1950s, it was known as Canfield's Big Rock Café. Moonshadows is a celebrity favorite and recently got quite a bit of press as the restaurant where Mel Gibson dined before his "arrest for drunk driving brouhaha." But it seems as though the spirits served at the restaurant bar aren't the only kind of spirits that the restaurant is famous for.

Several sources report that there are strange happenings in the restaurant's rest rooms. Water faucets in the women's rest room seem to have a life of their own and turn on and off by unseen hands, while in the men's room, a cloudy image of a ghost appears in the mirror. Although one of the restaurant's bartenders, who claims to be "old enough to be the ghost himself," says that these reported hauntings aren't true, I am more of the opinion that where there's smoke, there's fire, so next time you're in Malibu, stop by Moonshadows, have a great meal, and don't forget to use the restroom before you leave.

Twenty-Six Miles Across The Sea

Santa Catalina Island and the City of Avalon
Los Angles County, 90704

P eople have been living on Santa Catalina Island for at least 7,000 years. Archaeologists excavating on a limited scale at Little Harbor on the seaward side of the Island keep coming up with earlier and earlier dates. They find evidence of increasingly complex material cultures with a strong maritime adaptation. These earlier groups of peoples exploited the rich resources of the sea — from abalone and other mollusks, to small and large fish, and marine mammals such as sea lions.

The Island's more recent history spans time from the small villages of the Gabrielino Indians, through Spanish, then Mexican occupation. The Gabrielino/Tongva Tribes are renowned for their mining and the working and trading of soapstone which was found in great quantities and varieties on the Island. This material was in high demand and was traded up and down the California coast.

The first European to ever set foot on the island was the Portuguese explorer Juan Rodriguez Cabrillo, sailing for Spain in 1542. He claimed the island for Spain and christened it *San Salvador*. Another Spanish explorer, Sebastian Vizcaino, rediscovered the island on the eve of Saint Catherine's day, November 24, 1602. He renamed it *Santa Catalina* to honor the feast day of St. Catherine of Alexandria.

For the next 300 years, the island served as home or base of operation for all sorts of visitors, from Russian otter hunters to Spanish smugglers to Chinese pirates. Franciscan monks tried to build a mission there, but failed due to the lack of fresh water on the island.

In the 1860s, Catalina Island experienced a brief period of gold rush fever but no gold was found, and ultimately those early mining attempts were abandoned. By the end of the nineteenth century, the island was almost uninhabited except for a few cattle herders.

The first owner to try to develop the Island into a resort destination was George Shatto, a real estate speculator from Grand Rapids, Michigan, who purchased Catalina for $200,000 at the height of the real estate boom in Southern California in 1887. Shatto created the settlement that would become Avalon, and can be credited with building the town's first hotel, the original Hotel Metropole, and pier. His sister-in-law, Etta Whitney, came up with the name *Avalon*, which was pulled as a reference from Lord Alfred Tennyson's poem "Idylls of the King," which was about the legend of King Arthur. Despite Shatto's best efforts, in a few years time he had to default on his loan.

The sons of Phineas Banning bought the island in 1891 from the estate of James Lick and established the Santa Catalina Island Company to develop it as a resort. They built themselves a home on what is now Twin Harbors. Their efforts were set back on November 29, 1915, when a fire burned half of Avalon's buildings, including six hotels and several clubs. World War I also hampered tourism, and the Banning brothers were forced to sell the island.

William Wrigley, Jr. bought controlling interest in the Santa Catalina Island Company in 1919, and investing millions in both needed infrastructure and attractions. In 1921, he sold lots in the town of Avalon. The tourism industry was encouraged by the construction of a beautiful Art Deco dance hall, called the *Casino*, in 1929.

The Chicago Cubs, also owned by Wrigley, used the island for the team's spring training from 1920-1950. In 1936, Ronald Reagan, as a young radio announcer for WHO in Des Moines, Iowa, traveled to Catalina to cover the Cubs during spring training. While there, he took a screen test and was offered an acting role.

During World War II, the island was closed to tourists and used as a military training facility, and in the early 1940s during World War II, Marilyn Monroe, as a young, married woman, briefly lived in Avalon with her first husband, James Dougherty, a lieutenant in the Merchant Marine who was stationed on the island. Monroe often baby-sat for neighborhood children.

In 1975, Philip Wrigley deeded the Wrigley shares in the Santa Catalina Island Company to the Catalina Island Conservancy that he had helped create. The Conservancy now stewards eighty-eight percent of the island.

Catalina, which is technically a part of Los Angeles County, has had a unique relationship with Hollywood's filmmakers for almost a century. The Island has been immortalized on the silver screen hundreds of times and has been transformed into a variety of locales. One of the first "talkie" movies filmed on the Island was *Condemned,* starring Ronald Colman in 1929. The following years saw such classic films as *Island of Lost Souls* (1932), *Rain* (1932), *Treasure Island* (1933*), Captain Blood* (1935), *Mutiny on the Bounty* (1935), and *Captains Courageous* (1937) all being filmed on the Island. A small herd of Buffalo were brought in for a 1924 movie shoot and their ancestors, a herd of about 200, still roams the island interior.

The frequency of filming on the Island during this period introduced several of Hollywood's screen favorites to the charms of Santa Catalina, and many famous actors and celebrities were regularly spotted both on the Island and off the coast on their palatial yachts. Charlie Chaplin and his wife, Paulette Goddard, were frequent visitors and loved angling for marlin and tuna around the Island. James Cagney and his wife were known to anchor their yacht Marian in Descanso Bay. Cecil B. De Mille, who filmed at least three pictures on the Island, was quoted in *The Catalina Islander* as saying that Catalina is "the only place where I can get away to work amid real inspiration."

The Hotel St. Catherine ran a weekly column in the local newspaper called "Lobbying at the Hotel St. Catherine." Each week, Harry Grattan, proprietor of St. Catherine's gift shop, would report his celebrity sightings. Joan Crawford, Clark Gable, Betty Grable, Irving Thalberg, and Johnny Weismuller were all frequent visitors, and to this day, it seems that the ghosts of many of Catalina's former residents and visitors are reluctant to leave.

Catalina Visitors Country Club

At the Catalina Visitors Country Club, where the Cubs trained, a tall, thin, ghostly man wearing a baseball uniform and cap from the 1930s was seen by an employee who was closing up the Sports Bar facility in 1991. The ghost moved across the courtyard to another dining area on the other side of the patio then disappeared. There also seems to be an unknown ghost haunting the boiler room.

At the Casino, many people have reported incidents involving the women's restroom. Cold spots, a feeling of being watched, and mysterious noises that cannot be traced are frequent occurrences. There is also a definite cold spot in the Casino bar. Organ music is known to bellow out of the speaker system even when the power to the tape machine is off. People hear music and people talking near the stage area in the ballroom when nobody else is there. The theater is said to be haunted by a ghost who comes in and takes a seat during movies. The very-much-alive customers say they feel something brush against their legs, and then if they glance over to the empty seat next to them, there is an indentation in the seat cushion as if someone were actually sitting there.

The Hollyhill House

On the south side of Avalon, perched high in the hills sits The Hollyhill House. The Queen Anne style house was built in 1890 by Avalon pioneer Peter Gano. It is believed that Gano's spirit remains in the house to this day along with several others. Footsteps, doors slamming, and cold gusts of air are common at Hollyhill. The current owner of the home, which is a private residence, allows the Museum Society to give tours four times a year.

The Zane Grey Pueblo Hotel

The Zane Grey Pueblo Hotel, which was once the home of the prolific author, was constructed in 1926, and those that work there are certain that Mr. Grey's spirit is still around, although the paranormal activity seems to be stronger in the off-season months from December to April.

The Inn at Mt. Ada

The Inn at Mt. Ada, which was the former home of William Wrigley, Jr., and now is a Bed and Breakfast, and has it's share of spectral noises and phantom shadows that roam the grounds. A ghostly woman has been seen where the road to the Inn meets up with the main road, and in Room 4, a ghostly young woman appears out of nowhere, looks at the guests in their bed, then glides off to the closet door and vanishes.

The Banning House Lodge

The Banning House Lodge was built in 1910, and is located on the isthmus of Catalina Island at Two Harbors. The lodge is perched on a hilltop with sweeping views of both Isthmus Cove and Catalina Harbor. A ghostly figure dubbed the "White Lady" has often been spotted here. Others have reported the smells of tobacco and fish that reportedly come from the spirit of an old fisherman.

Von's Market

Many other private houses on the Island have their share of hauntings and even the Von's Market boasts a couple of resident spirits of employees who used to work there.

Avalon Cemetery

Winstead "Doodles" Weaver

Avalon cemetery is where comedian Winstead "Doodles" Weaver is buried. He was the brother of NBC-TV executive Sylvester "Pat" Weaver and the uncle of actress Sigourney Weaver. In the 1940s he was a prominent member of Spike Jones' band, The City Slickers, and is well remembered for his routine of a frantic and corny call of a horse race ("William Tell Overture"): "It's Girdle in the stretch! Locomotive is on the rail! Apartment House is second with plenty of room! It's Cabbage by a head!" and so on, segueing into an impression of the gravelly-voiced Clem McCarthy who forgets whether he's covering a horse race or a boxing match. The race features an apparent nag called "Feitlebaum," who begins at long odds, runs almost the entire race a distant last, and suddenly emerges as the winner.

After his days with The City Slickers, Weaver hosted humorous children-oriented TV shows, and played eccentric characters in various guest appearances on other shows. Weaver had a lifelong battle with alcoholism and faced declining health in his later years. He committed suicide by gunshot at age 72. It's been said that Weaver was very approachable in later years and loved to chat with fans—a policy that no doubt continues to this day at his gravesite.

John "Chicken Johnny" Brinkley

Another colorful personality buried at Avalon Cemetery is John "Chicken Johnny" Brinkley (1844-1936). *Chicken Johnny* was a hermit who lived in a shack towards the back of Avalon Canyon. He raised chickens and sold eggs to the local population until his death at the ripe old age of ninety. Several years later, John was immortalized in a painting by renowned local artist Roger "Bud" Upton (1900-1988). Upton, a founding father of the Catalina Art Association painted in Avalon longer than any other artist to date, and thorough his art, recorded buildings and landmarks of the time, as well as everyday life on the Island. Upton's ashes are also resting in peace at Avalon Cemetery. Every so often, people swear that they've seen the ghost of Chicken Johnny still selling his eggs on the island he loved.

Jinxed Productions?

Many Hollywood films are famous for "carrying a curse." While some of the stories related to these productions seem to be made up by eager publicists attempting to draw in big box office bucks, many of these tales cannot be dismissed as sheer coincidence.

The Exorcist Curse

A story widely believed to be true has director William Friedkin supposedly asking technical advisor Reverend Thomas Bermingham to exorcise the set. The Reverend refused, saying an exorcism might increase anxiety. This probably did not happen because, according to Catholic doctrine, an exorcism has to be applied for and approved by Church authorities; and since this information was written into the Exorcist script, Friedkin would have known that. So instead of an exorcism, Reverend Bermingham reportedly visited the set, gave a blessing with holy water, and spoke briefly to reassure the cast and crew.

Other accounts about ominous events surrounding the year-long shoot include the deaths of nine people associated with the production and stories about a mysterious fire that destroyed the set one weekend. These are probably folklore, and both *Exorcist* author William Peter Blatty and actor Max von Sydow are said to have discounted such tales as nonsense. So maybe it's just a strange coincidence that actress Linda Blair injured her back when a piece of the rig broke during one of the scenes where she was thrown about on the bed. Or that Ellen Burstyn received a permanent spinal injury during the filming of a sequence where she is thrown away from her possessed daughter. (A harness jerked her hard away from the bed, she fell on her coccyx and screamed out. The painful scene was left in the movie.) What about the fact that two actors that appeared in the film, Jack MacGowran and Vasiliki Maliaros both died before the film was released or that Christian evangelist Billy Graham claimed that an actual demon was living in the celluloid reels of the movie? We'll probably never know.

The Cursed Rebels

James Dean

All three of the main stars of the movie *Rebel Without a Cause*, James Dean, Natalie Wood, and Sal Mineo died relatively young under tragic circumstances and therein lies the curse.

Dean was killed in a traffic accident in Cholame, California, on September 30, 1955, at the age of 24. Because of his fondness for auto racing, Dean purchased the ill-fated 1955 Porsche Spyder sports car in which he died, because he planned to drive it in an upcoming race in Salinas, California, on October 1, 1955. Ironically, he was issued a speeding ticket only two hours and fifteen minutes before his fatal accident. Years later, the famous Failure Analysis Associates, from Menlo Park, California, reconstructed and re-created all details of the accident at the same approximate time on September 30th, and have concluded that James Dean was traveling 55 to 56 m.p.h. when the fateful accident occurred, thereby proving he had not been speeding after all. Adding insult to fatal injury, Dean filmed a highway safety commercial with actor Gig Young on the set of *Giant* just two months before he was killed. Dean told Young, "I used to fly around quite a bit, took a lot of unnecessary chances on the highway. Now when I drive on the highway, I'm extra cautious." The commercial ended with Dean saying, "And remember, drive safely, because the life you save may be mine."

Natalie Wood

I'm frightened to death of the water," said Dean's co-star Natalie Wood in a long ago interview. "I can swim a little bit, but I'm afraid of water that is dark." As if to prove the point, during the filming of the movie *This Property is Condemned*, she was so scared of performing a skinny-dipping scene, that co-star Robert Redford held her feet underwater to help steady her while shooting it. And when she made *Splendor in the Grass,* director Elia Kazan had to lie and trick her into doing the scenes at the water reservoir.

Natalie's worst fear caught up with her on the night of November 29, 1981, when she drowned off Catalina Island at the age of forty-three. Wood was on board her yacht, *Splendor,* with husband Robert Wagner and actor Christopher Walken. There were reports saying that Wagner and Walken had a loud argument about Walken's behavior towards Natalie, and Wood apparently tried to either leave the yacht or secure a dinghy that was banging against the hull when she accidentally slipped and fell overboard. A woman on shore said she heard cries for help from the water that night, along with voices replying "We're coming." Wagner, Walken, and the pilot of the boat said they heard nothing.

Sal Mineo

Another *Rebel* star, Sal Mineo, was brutally murdered outside his West Hollywood apartment on February 12, 1976, at the age of thirty-seven. Many bizarre rumors floated around about his murder, but when his killer, Lionel Ray Williams, was caught, he turned out to be a drug-addled seventeen-year-old who had no idea who Mineo was and was only interested in the money he had on him.

Nick Adams

Actor Nick Adams is often linked to the urban legend surrounding this film as well. Adams, often considered "The Poor Man's James Dean," attempted to let the spirit of Dean live vicariously through him in his work, which was notably most successful with the TV series *The Rebel*. But following an Oscar nomination for the film *Twilight of Honor*, Adams' career began to decline and he allegedly died of a drug overdose on February 7, 1968, at the age of thirty-six, although several people, including his own daughter, believe he may have been murdered.

Rebel Ghosts and Curses

It is said that the ghost of Sal Mineo now haunts the carport behind the apartment building where he was murdered, and residents on Catalina Island claim that Natalie Wood's spirit is often seen near the location of her drowning.

While there are no regular sightings of James Dean himself, the mangled wreckage of his death car seems to have taken on a grisly life of its own.

George Barris, one of the best-known designers of custom cars in the world, bought the wrecked car to use it for parts. While the 1955 Porsche was being downloaded from the wrecker, it fell and broke a mechanic's leg.

Two doctors bought the engine and drive train to use in their race cars. One of the doctors died in an accident and the other was seriously injured in an accident as well.

The garage that was home to James Dean's cursed car and where other California Highway Patrol cars were kept for the exhibit caught on fire mysteriously. All the cars were destroyed except for the 1955 silver gray Porsche Spyder.

There are dozens of other cursed car stories, but it is said that during a ride to Los Angeles packed in a crate in 1960, the silver gray 1955 Porsche Spyder completely vanished, and to this day, no one knows what happened to the cursed car that took James Dean's life.

The Poltergeist Curse

The Poltergeist curse supposedly attached to all of the *Poltergeist* motion pictures and its stars and is a superstition based on the information that five of the cast members from these movies died, and two of these five died at a young age (twelve and twenty-two).

Dominique Dunne, the twenty-two-year-old actress who played the oldest sister, Dana, in the first movie died after being choked by a jealous boyfriend in 1982. Dunne died on November 4, 1982, at Cedars-Sinai Medical Center in Los Angeles, four days after her boyfriend choked her into a coma from which she never awoke. Weeks earlier, Dunne had ended her abusive live-in relationship with Los Angeles chef John Sweeney. On the night of October 30, 1982, Sweeny dropped by their former shared residence to plead with her to take him back. The conversation did not go as he'd hoped and the encounter ended with him strangling her for what was later determined to be four to six minutes, then leaving her for dead in her driveway. Sweeney was convicted of voluntary manslaughter, sentenced in November, 1983, and released in 1986 after serving only three years, eight months of a six and one half year sentence.

After he was released, Sweeny became head chef at a restaurant in Santa Monica, California, called The Chronicle. Dunne's family and friends, who did not feel justice was served by his light jail sentence, took justice into their own hands, so to speak. Learning that Sweeny was working at the restaurant, they began handing out notices to people in and around the eatery that read: "The hands that prepared your food strangled Dominique Dunne on October 30, 1982." Sweeny lost his job because of this, then changed his name to John Maura and moved out of California.

Heather O'Rourke, the twelve-year-old actress who played Carol Anne in the three *Poltergeist* movies, died of septic shock on February 1, 1988, at the Children's Hospital in San Diego. What had been thought to be a bout of ordinary flu, launched her into cardiac arrest during the drive to the local hospital as bacterial toxins set loose by a bowel obstruction made their way into her bloodstream. Her heart was successfully restarted and she was flown by helicopter to the much-larger Children's Hospital where she underwent an operation to remove the obstruction. The toxins proved too much, and she died on the operating table. The year before her death, she'd been diagnosed as having Crohn's Disease, a lifelong inflammatory small bowel disease which often first manifests in children and young adults

Actor Julian Beck who played Kane in Poltergeist II: The Other Side, died of stomach cancer, with which he was diagnosed with before he had accepted the role. He was sixty years old.

Actor Will Sampson, who played Taylor the Medicine Man in Poltergeist II, died of postoperative kidney failure and pre-operative malnutrition problems after receiving a heart-lung transplant six weeks earlier at the age of fifty-three.

Brian Gibson, fifty-nine years old, director of *Poltergeist II*, died January 4, 2004 from Ewing's Sarcoma.

Other legends surrounding the films have pointed to a potential cause of the curse. The most widely blamed alleges that real human skeletal remains were used as props in the first film, causing the angry spirits of the deceased to wreak havoc. Actress JoBeth Williams has said in interviews (most notably the *E! True Hollywood Story* episode *The Curse of Poltergeist*) that she was actually told that the skeletons used in the well-known swimming pool scene in the first *Poltergeist* film were real.

Other occurrences that have been attributed to the curse include:

The "Freeling" home in Southern California where the original film was partially shot was damaged by the Northridge earthquake in 1994.

During a photography session for *Poltergeist III*, it was discovered that one shot of co-star Zelda Rubenstein had shining light obstructing the view of her face. Rubenstein claims the photo was taken at the moment her real-life mother died.

JoBeth Williams, who played the mother, Diane Freeling, claims she returned home from the set each day to find pictures on her wall askew. She would straighten them, only to find them crooked again the next day.

During a scene when Robbie Freeling (Oliver Robins) was choked by a clown in his room, something went wrong with the prop and Robins was actually being choked. Director Steven Spielberg praised him for his authenticity until he caught on that the actor was, in fact, not acting and rushed to save him.

James Khan who wrote the novelization of the movie claims that one night, as he typed the words "Thunder and lightning ripped the sky," a blast of lightning hit his building and blew the cover off an air conditioning unit with enough force to hit him in the back.

During the making of *Poltergeist III*, a movie set of a parking garage was completely engulfed by fire during shooting of a fire scene, from which only one crew member escaped without a scratch.

An RKO Radioactive Picture

In 1955, John Wayne promised to make a film directed by Dick Powell, and visited the RKO studios to discuss possible projects. When he arrived at the studio, he happened to pick up a screenplay called *The Conqueror,* which had accidentally been left on Powell's desk. After reading through it, Wayne liked the script so much that he insisted on taking on the starring role as Genghis Khan.

During a thirteen-week location shoot in Snow Canyon in the Utah desert near Yucca Flats, the site of recent nuclear testing where eleven atomic bombs had recently been detonated, the cast and crew were exposed to residual contaminated nuclear fallout. To make matters worse, after the location shooting was completed, sixty tons of the toxic dirt from the site was unwittingly transported back to Hollywood in order to match interior shooting done there.

Over the next two decades, nearly 100 of the film's 200 cast and crew members developed forms of cancer, many more than the normal percentage of a random group of this size. Quite a few died from cancer or cancer-related problems. John Wayne died of lung cancer, Susan Hayward of malignant brain tumors, Pedro Armendáriz (who shot himself to death soon after learning he had terminal kidney cancer) and Agnes Moorehead, who also died of lung cancer. Thomas Gomez and John Hoyt also contacted the "Big C" as did director Dick Powell, who died of stomach cancer. These figures do not include several hundred local American Indians who served as extras on the film, nor did it include relatives who had visited cast and crew members on the set. An article written in *People Magazine* in 1980 quoted the reaction of a scientist from the Pentagon's Defense Nuclear Agency to the news. He said, "Please, God, don't let us have killed John Wayne."

Eccentric billionaire Howard Hughes provided the financial backing for this film and later paid an extra $12 million (estimated) for every existing print of it out of a sense of guilt. You see, it was he who paid for the shipping of the radioactive dirt to Hollywood for retakes. He kept a jealous hold on the film, not even allowing it to be seen on television, for seventeen years until 1974, when Paramount managed to secure the rights to reissue it.

While the Utah desert may not be a great place to haunt, the ghost of John Wayne is said to walk the decks of his beloved yacht, *The Wild Goose*, which is docked in Southern California's Newport Beach Harbor. Several maintenance workers, passers by, and Mrs. Wayne have seen the spirit of the actor walking the decks of his beloved yacht, or waving from the top deck.

The Our Gang Curse

It could be sheer coincidence, but it seems as though an unusually high percentage of the child actors who starred in the *Our Gang* film series have met with tragic ends.

Carl Switzer (Alfalfa) was shot to death at age thirty-one over a $50 debt and Darla Hood Our Gang's leading lady contracted hepatitis and died at age forty-seven. Both are buried not far from each other at the Hollywood Forever Cemetery.

Three hundred-pound Norman (Chubby) Chaney suffered from a glandular ailment in early adulthood. In 1935, he had an operation for his condition and his weight dropped to 136 pounds. Sadly, he never recovered, and passed away at the age of eighteen.

William Thomas (Buckwheat) did not die tragically, but he did die young of a heart attack, at the age forty-nine, and Kendall McCormas, known as Breezy Brisbane, committed suicide at the age of sixty-four.

William Robert Laughline (Froggy) was killed in a motor scooter accident when he was hit by a truck at age sixteen.

Mathew Beard (Stymie) led a life of crime and drugs. He suffered a stroke, then contracted pneumonia and died at age fifty-six.

Scotty Beckett went on to star in other films after leaving *Our Gang*. As an adult he checked into a Hollywood nursing home on May 8, 1968, in need of medical attention after suffering a serious beating. He died two days later. Although pills and a note were found, no conclusion was made by the coroner as to the exact cause of his death. He was just thirty-eight years old.

Robert Hutchins (Wheezer) had joined the Air Corps and was killed at the age of nineteen when his plane crash landed during a training exercise.

Pete the Pup was poisoned by an unknown assailant.

Darwood Kaye (Waldo) had a successful career in show business after the series ended and then joined the ministry, but was killed by a hit-and-run driver at age seventy-two.

Robert Blake (Mickey) is still alive and had a very long and successful career in show business, but TVs Baretta made headlines when he was arrested in April 2002 for the murder of his wife. He was acquitted at trial in March 2005.

Kendall McComas (Breezy Brisbane) committed suicide just a few weeks short of his sixty-fifth birthday.

Committing Kryptonite

In Hollywood-speak, "Committing Kryptonite" is what superstitious types believe can happen to a person's life after being associated with *Superman*.

George Reeves

George Reeves, who played "The Man of Steel" in the 1951 film *Superman and the Mole Men* and the following TV series *The Adventures of Superman*, suffered from typecasting syndrome and found it difficult to find other acting jobs after the TV series ended. A heavy drinker, George had threatened suicide many times. One night during a party at his home in 1959, he went upstairs alone and moments later, a single shot rang out. Whether it was suicide or murder is anybody's guess as the case has still not been solved, but one thing is for sure. While Reeves' alter ego was faster than a speeding bullet, the actor was not.

Reeves' house in Benedict Canyon is said to be quite haunted by the ghost of Reeves who is probably trying to come back and tell the world the actual facts of his demise, but it seems as though no one has stayed around long enough to listen. One couple saw Reeves materialize in his old bedroom, fully outfitted in his Superman costume and then watched as he slowly faded away. They moved out of the house that same night. A number of subsequent owners have also reported strange goings on at the house which is probably the reason the house has had quite a number of tenants since that fateful day in 1959.

Christopher Reeve

Christopher Reeve, who played the Man of Steel in four *Superman* films between 1978 and 1987, was paralyzed in a horse-riding accident on May 27, 1995. Reeve died of heart failure on October 10, 2004, after being a quadriplegic for almost a decade. His widow Dana, a non-smoker, was diagnosed with lung cancer in August 2005, and she died in March 2006, aged forty-four years, leaving their son Will an orphan at the age of thirteen.

Margo Kidder

Margot Kidder played Lois Lane in four of the films. In 1996, she had a nervous breakdown and went missing for several days. When she was found, her dentures were gone, her hair had been hacked off with a razor blade, and she had no recollection of her missing days, and yet, she still denounces the theory of the "curse."

Richard Pryor

It is said that Richard Pryor, who played a villain in *Superman III*, and had a long history of drug abuse, had an affair with Kidder which supposedly ended his marriage. When he was later diagnosed with multiple sclerosis, he asked his ex-wife to return to him, and she nursed him until his death from a heart attack in 2005. Pryor's widow believes in the "curse" and says that if she was one of the films' producers, she would hire a voodoo princess to remove it.

Marlon Brando

Marlon Brando, who played Superman's father Jor-El in *Superman: The Movie*, had a tragic family life. He outlived his daughter Cheyenne, who committed suicide; and his son Christian was sentenced to ten years in jail after pleading guilty to voluntary manslaughter. Christian shot his half-sister Cheyenne's lover, causing Cheyenne to later hang herself.

Lee Quigley

Lee Quigley (1976-1991) played the part of the infant Kal-El who was sent from Krypton to Earth by his parents at the beginning of *Superman: The Movie*. When Lee's parents split up a few years later, he went to live with his grandparents in London. As a teenager, the young man developed a liking for glue-sniffing, and died from solvent abuse at age for fourteen.

Rob Burnett, Adam Robitel, and Todd Stanley

While filming *Superman Returns* in 2006, Producer Rob Burnett was mugged by a gang of four men who broke his ribs and blacked his eye. Editor Adam Robitel damaged his spine and punctured a lung after falling through a window, and cameraman Todd Stanley suffered a skull fracture and the loss of the tip of his finger when he fell down some stairs.

It took sixteen years to find a new Superman because several of Hollywood's best candidates turned down the starring role. Ashton Kutcher, for example, said no after deciding his life was too good to risk invoking the "curse."

It's worth noting that the director of the first Superman film was Richard Donner, fresh from filming another cursed film, *The Omen*.

The Omen

The Omen was originally released in 1976 and starred Gregory Peck and Lee Remick. As part of its pre-release publicity campaign, and to point out the significance of "the three sixes" as The Sign of Satan, the movie was sneak-previewed nationwide in the USA on the 6th of June in 1976. Initially entitled *The Antichrist* then *The Birthmark*, the film seemed to fall victim to a sinister curse.

Gregory Peck, David Seltzer, and Mace Neufeld

Actor Gregory Peck and screenwriter David Seltzer took separate planes to the United Kingdom for filming the movie, yet both of their planes were struck by lightning over the Atlantic. A few weeks later, executive producer Mace Neufeld also left Los Angeles for the UK, and if you think lightning doesn't strike thrice, think again. Neufeld later commented, "That was the roughest five minutes I've ever had on an airliner." Not long after that, producer Harvey Bernhard was on location in Rome, and lightning just missed him. And that was just the tip of the iceberg.

The hotel in which Neufeld and his wife were staying was bombed by the IRA. So, too, was a restaurant where the executives and actors, including Peck, were expected for dinner on November 12th.

The Crew

On day one of the shoot, several principal members of the crew survived a head-on car crash. Then a plane they had been due to hire for aerial filming was switched to another client at the last minute and crashed on takeoff, killing all on board. Rottweilers hired for the film attacked their trainers, a tiger handler died in a freak accident, and the curse continued into post-production of the film.

On a Friday the 13th in 1976, special-effects designer John Richardson, fresh from masterminding a brutal decapitation scene in *The Omen* skidded into a collision that left his assistant, who was in the passenger seat, sliced in half. Her injuries bore an uncanny resemblance to the ones he had prepared for the movie. To make matters even spookier, a road sign at the scene of the accident, marking the distance to an otherwise insignificant Dutch town read: Ommen, 66.6 km.

Stuntman Alf Joint went to work on *A Bridge Too Far* after working on *The Omen,* but was badly injured and hospitalized when a stunt went wrong. He only had to jump from a roof onto an airbag, an easy stunt for someone with his experience, but this time, something odd happened. He appeared to fall suddenly and awkwardly. When he woke up in hospital, he told friends it felt like he had been pushed.

During an interview in 2004, Father Jason Spadafore, a Roman Catholic bishop who has performed three real-life exorcisms, issued the following warning to any actor signing up for a horror movie: "Any time that you so much as pretend to call upon a demon, there is a chance a demon is going to come up and make its presence known. I would tell them to be very careful ... if they were Catholic, I would tell them to pray a rosary or wear a cross, cross yourself with holy water every day, do something to protect yourself because you are going into potentially dangerous territory. For somebody who is non-Catholic, I'd tell them to go to whomever their cleric is, whether it be their minister, their rabbi, their Lama, whomever. They need to find out whatever spiritual protections are available, and use them."

Rosemary's Baby

The unsettling novel by Ira Levin that deals with a woman being raped and impregnated by the devil and giving birth to the "Devil's spawn" was first published in 1967, the year after a public announcement regarding the founding of the Church of Satan by Anton La Vey. The film, released in 1968 and directed by Roman Polanski, was apparently a joy to LeVay who was quoted as saying that it was "the best paid commercial for Satanism since the Inquisition," and saw it as contributing to the growth of his church.

Mia Farrow and Frank Sinatra

The movie also has contributed some interesting coincidences regarding members of the cast and crew; the least of which being that Mia Farrow received divorce papers from then-husband Frank Sinatra during the filming of _Rosemary's Baby_.

Robert Kennedy

On June 5, 1968, ten days before _Rosemary's Baby_ was released, Polanski and his wife, Sharon Tate, dined with Robert Kennedy in Malibu. Shortly afterward, Kennedy left for the Ambassador Hotel in Los Angeles, where he was assassinated.

William Castle and Krzysztof Komeda

In April 1969, days after receiving death threats and hate mail relating to the film, producer William Castle was rushed into hospital with kidney failure. At one point, he supposedly cried out "Rosemary, for God's sake drop that knife." As he convalesced, he discovered that Krzysztof Komeda, the Polish composer who wrote the score for the film and an old friend of Polanski's and Tate's, was in the same hospital. Komeda died of a brain clot before the month was out. His death strangely echoed that of Rosemary's friend, Hutch, in the film.

Sharon Tate

A year after its release, Polanski's wife, Sharon Tate, was murdered by the Manson Family. Tate was pregnant with the couple's first child when she died.

John Lennon

John Lennon lived in the Manhattan apartment building called The Dakota where *Rosemary's Baby* was filmed. He was murdered in front of the building in 1980, and is said to haunt the area around the undertakers gate. But Lennon isn't the building's only blithe spirit. In the sixties, the ghost of a young boy/young man was seen by a couple of construction workers at The Dakota. A girl dressed in turn-of-the-century clothing was seen by painters working at the building several years later.

Twilight Zone: The Movie

It would be hard to find a movie that rivals *Twilight Zone* for one of the most grisly tragedies in filmmaking history.

Vic Morrow, Rene Chen, and Myca Dinh Le

In the early the morning hours of July 23, 1982, actor Vic Morrow and two child co-stars were killed while filming a scene from the movie just outside of Los Angeles in Indian Dunes. Over the years, the Dunes had been used as a location for many movies and television programs starting in the days of silent films and westerns. In recent years, *Black Sheep Squadron* with Robert Conrad and *Some Kind Of Hero* with the late Richard Pryor were filmed there. The last television series to use that location was *China Beach*.

During the fatal scene, Vic Morrow's character was attempting to save two children from the Viet Cong by carrying them across a man-made river. A helicopter was hovering low over a make-believe Vietnamese village when an explosive charge from the special effects hit the tail rotor of the helicopter sending it crashing to the ground. One child, Rene Chen, was crushed to death by the right skid. Vic Morrow and the other child, Myca Dinh Le, were decapitated. Criminal charges against the production company were eventually dismissed in a much-publicized trial.

Steven Spielberg, the film's Executive Producer was later quoted as saying, "No movie is worth dying for. If something isn't safe, it's the right and responsibility of every actor and crew member to yell "cut." Unfortunately, the accident happened so fast, that nobody could.

A Handful of Haunted Hotels

The Beverly Hills Hotel — 9641 Sunset Boulevard
The Beverly Hills Hotel is a luxury, five-star hotel, located on Sunset Boulevard in the center of Beverly Hills. It is surrounded by twelve acres of lush, tropical gardens, exotic flowers, and private walkways. Once the happy hunting grounds of people like Howard Hughes, John F. Kennedy, and John Lennon, the Beverly Hills Hotel was constructed by Burton Green in 1912, and helped jump start the fame of glamorous Beverly Hills. Its bungalows are said to be haunted by several ghosts including Rachmaninoff and Harpo Marx. The lobby is said to be haunted by actor Peter Finch who suffered a fatal heart attack there. Finch is buried at Hollywood Forever Cemetery just a few steps away from Rudolph Valention

Chateau Marmont — 8221 Sunset Boulevard
Modeled after an elegant Loire Valley castle, the Chateau Marmont is a landmark from the 1920s-era Hollywood that has served as a home away from home to every legend from every era of Hollywood history. Built in the late 1920s as an apartment house, the chateau was later converted into a hotel. Its early guest list included Jean Harlow, Bette Davis, Errol Flynn, Stan Laurel, and John Wayne. In the '60s and '70s, the Marmont drew leading rock and folk stars, from Mick Jagger to Joan Baez. Although well known for its privacy, the Marmont made international headlines when comedian John Belushi died of an overdose in Bungalow 2.

The hotel's rooms, hallways, and bungalows are said to be haunted by a number of well-known Hollywood spirits, one of which has even been known to climb into guest's beds in the middle of the night. Every kind of phenomena has been witnessed here and the place is so creepy that it is considered one of the most haunted hotels in the United States.

The Oban Hotel — 6364 Yucca Street
Now called The Hollywood Guest Inn, many celebs, including Glenn Miller, Marilyn Monroe, and Orson Wells stayed at this hotel in its heyday. It is said to be haunted by the ghost of a stuntman and double for actor Harry Langdon. His name is Charles Lowe, and he committed suicide

there in 1933. He is joined in his afterlife performances by several other unidentified spirits including a few other male ghosts, a female ghost, and a very sinister presence in the basement.

The Hollywood Roosevelt Hotel — 7000 Hollywood Boulevard
Named after President Theodore Roosevelt, the Hollywood Roosevelt opened in a gala ceremony on May 15, 1927, by its owners Douglas Fairbanks and his wife, Mary Pickford, and movie mogul Louis B. Meyer. The luxury hotel was designed to serve the new movie industry, and in keeping with that theme, the first Academy Award ceremony was held in the hotel's Blossom Room in 1929. The motion picture Academy held their meetings there from 1927 to 1935.

Over the years, the Roosevelt has continued to host the most prestigious movie stars of the day. In both 1984 and again in 2005, the hotel underwent extensive restorations, and since then, the Roosevelt ghosts have been putting in frequent appearances.

One of the most common paranormal occurrences happens at the front desk on a regular basis. Ghostly guests have been known to ring the switchboard from rooms that have since been remodeled and no longer exist.

In the Blossom Room, it's been reported that a little girl spirit, called Caroline, is said to be searching for her mother, and the figure of a very agitated man is often seen walking back and forth, as if on a mission. There is also a cold spot at one end of the room that never goes away. Some paranormal researchers believe that it is a portal to the other side where spirits come in and out at will.

Montgomery Clift
Actor Montgomery Clift stayed in room 928 during the making of *From Here to Eternity*, and rumor has it, you can still hear him practicing his bugle in the hall that leads to that room. Many unknowing guests staying in room 928 have called downstairs to the front desk in the middle of the night to complain about the racket.

Marilyn Monroe
Early in her modeling career, Marilyn Monroe lived in one of the cabanas next to the swimming pool which contained a beautiful full-length mirror. The mirror is now hanging in the main building where some say they still see her image gazing back at them. Monroe also posed on the diving board of the hotel's swimming pool for her first print ad, and there are many reports of seeing her ghost on a lounge chair near the pool reenacting that photo shoot.

Clark Gable and Carole Lombard

It appears that the three-floor penthouse suite, where Clark Gable and Carole Lombard once secretly trysted before going public with their love seems to hold a place in the hearts of these ill-fated lovebirds because there are frequent reports that their ghosts come back every so often to relive those tender moments.

Harry Lee

Strangely enough, one tragic incident at the hotel back in the 1930s hasn't resulted in any sort of paranormal sightings. On December 8, 1932, an actor by the name of Harry Lee jumped to his death from one of the hotel's fire escapes and landed on the roof of the third floor wing. Perhaps he was happy to leave this life and doesn't choose to return to the scene of his demise.

Several years ago, I decided to spend the night at the Roosevelt, alone, to see if anything paranormal might occur. I checked into a small, cozy room on the eighth floor, ordered room service, and then settled in for the night. While I can't say that I saw or heard anything out of the ordinary, I couldn't shake the feeling that I wasn't alone. It felt as though someone was watching me the whole time I was there, especially in the bathroom. I pretty much slept with one eye open the whole night (with the bathroom light on) and eagerly checked out quite early the next morning.

Interestingly enough, when Chris Fleming stayed in the Montgomery Clift room (which was just upstairs from the room where I stayed) during the filming of an episode of *Dead Famous*, he heard quite a few noises in the bathroom and commented that he didn't like the feel of that bathroom either.

The Georgian Hotel —1415 Ocean Ave, Santa Monica, CA

The vintage Georgian Hotel opened in the beach community of Santa Monica in 1933, and was originally named The Lady Windemere. It was one of the first "skyscrapers" along a then sparsely populated Ocean Avenue.

The Art Deco style building was the coastal getaway to the stars who trekked in from Hollywood and Beverly Hills in the 1930s and 40s, and was a place where patrons could enjoy alcoholic spirits during the Prohibition Era. Regulars such as Clark Gable, Fatty Arbuckle, Carol Lombard, and other Hollywood stars would visit the hotel on weekends to unwind from the grind of filmmaking.

In the 1940s and 50s, Santa Monica was experiencing a technological and industrial business boom led by the growing Donald Douglas Aircraft manufacturing facility, so in addition to Hollywood stars, The Georgian became a temporary home to aircraft designers, servicemen who were put up in local hotels during World War II, and gamblers who would travel off shore for the evening to play at large casino barges anchored a few miles away in Santa Monica Bay.

In the late 60s, The Georgian reinvented itself as a modern, upscale apartment residence with unheard of amenities like a "bathroom in each room." Tenant and First Mother Rose Kennedy would often spend summers at The Georgian entertaining politicos, Hollywood royalty, and journalists in the lobby and on the dramatic verandah overlooking the Palisades and the Pacific beyond.

Today, the hotel still attracts the Hollywood elite. Oliver Stone, Robert DeNiro, and California Governor Arnold Schwarzenegger all enjoy the hotel's amenities along with ghosts of the past who still seem to linger as well.

The Red Griffin room in the hotel's basement was used as a speakeasy during Prohibition and is said to be haunted by dozens of celebrity ghosts. Their pictures hang on the red flocked wallpaper walls above the red leather banquettes. In an otherwise empty restaurant, employees have heard loud sighs or gasps, and disembodied voices calling out "Good Morning" is a common occurrence. At other times the sounds of running footsteps are heard throughout the restaurant when no one is there and a number of transparent apparitions have been seen.

One Final Note

Marilyn Monroe once said,

"Hollywood is a place where they'll pay you a thousand dollars for a kiss and fifty cents for your soul."

Maybe that's why many of the city's most restless spirits are still around. They're either looking for their lost souls or perhaps trying hard to redeem them in the afterlife.

Whatever the case may be, it's a certainly that in Hollywood, the show still goes on...and fortunately, unlike most tourist destinations, the price of admission is not measured in dollars and cents. All it takes to encounter our dearly departed is an open mind, a little bit of effort, and every so often, nerves of steel.

Are you game?

Contributors

David Wells

David Wells says he had a very ordinary family upbringing in a small Scottish village. His mother worked in a knitwear factory and his father was a coal miner. At the age of sixteen, he joined The Royal Navy, left when he was twenty-four, and began a career in catering within hotels and leisure clubs. In 1991, David decided to go back to college to study leisure as a career, and to fund this he was working forty hours a week as a chef and a waiter in a small hotel in the south of England.

While on Christmas Holiday in Scotland in 1992, David wound up in the hospital, severely ill with pneumonia. As he tells it, "On the second night in hospital I found myself in the corridor being told to go back to bed by an old lady. She said that this is not my time and I have work to do. I did as she asked only to find I was already there! Thinking nothing more than I had been dreaming, I forgot the incident and was released a few days later when improvements to my health were great enough. I returned to England and was convalescing when I started to experience odd happenings in my home, so odd that I found it impossible to sleep and was looking not so fresh. A friend suggested that I visit a woman who 'knew about these things' and I duly did."

He then went on to learn astrology to ground his abilities, which were showing themselves at an alarming rate. His memory of talking to relatives that had passed over when he was a child came back and he realized that being a psychic medium was his true vocation.

David is currently seen on the television show *Most Haunted* on The Travel Channel here in the U.S. and on *LivingTV* in the United Kingdom. He is the author of *David Wells' Complete Guide To Developing Your Psychic Skills* and a second book on the subject of past lives.

Barry Conrad

Barry Conrad originally hails from Hamilton, Ohio. When Conrad was twelve years old, he overheard a friend of his mother's discussing the paranormal incidents taking place in her new home on the outskirts of Fairfield, Ohio. Doors would slam shut of their own accord, objects moved around and the all pervasive odor of smoke would some- times filter through the house. One night, her son nearly jumped from the balcony of an upstairs bedroom, feeling that he was being asphyxiated by an invisible fire. Barry was impressed by the woman's apparent sincerity and that lead to his interest in supernatural matters.

He worked as a TV news cameraman at WKRC-TV in Cincinnati work- ing under the auspices of anchorman/reporter Nick Clooney (father of actor George Clooney), and in 1986, Barry moved to California to start his own production company called American Video Features (now known as Barcon Video).

During the fall of 1987, Conrad met Dr. Barry Taff who had once investigated a woman's claims that she had been raped and attacked by an invisible force. The story became a motion picture in 1983 called *The Entity*. Thereafter, Taff and Conrad developed a working relationship that lasts to this day, as they have investigated dozens of haunted house and poltergeist cases in the Los Angeles area.

In 1989, one of those cases turned out to be nearly as frightening as *The Entity*. While checking into a woman's story in San Pedro of malevolent ghostly activity, including the sighting of a disembodied head, the pair encountered violent phenomena. Conrad filmed the case and later made it into a documentary titled *An Unknown Encounter*. Segments of the story later appeared in an anthology film that he produced in 2002 called *California's Most Haunted*. Both shows garnered high ratings when they aired on the Sci-Fi Channel's *Tuesday De-classified* series in 2003.

Chris Fleming

Born in 1967 to Patricia Fleming and Blackhawks Hockey star Reggie Fleming, Chris spent the majority of his childhood in the Northwest suburbs of Chicago. From an early age, Chris was prone to experiencing extraordinary encounters with ghosts and other unexplained phenomenon. While some of the events can be classified as divine intervention, there were others that, to this day, Chris still considers terrifying.

Over the years, Chris has been a guest on numerous radio and television talk shows all around the world talking about his personal experiences with the paranormal. For the past three years, he has been the co-host of the popular TV show *Dead Famous* where he joins co-host Gail Porter in searching for celebrity ghosts across America, not only at the gravesites, but also in some of the most haunted locations in the USA. The show is broadcast in over fifteen countries, including the networks: *Bravo* in Canada, *Living TV* in The UK, and on *The Biography Channel* in the US. With three seasons and thirty-one episodes, Chris has captured thousands of EVP's (Electronic Voice Phenomena), unexplainable photos, and video footage that he believes can prove the existence of ghosts.

Chris is currently broadcasting his own podcast show titled *Spirit Talk*, and has recently begun writing one of many books he hopes to publish on his own personal paranormal experiences and insights into the other side. He hopes his experiences will help people understand who we are and why we are here. He also helms *Unknown Magazine* and is currently working on a new paranormal television show.

Kenny Kingston

Legendary celebrity psychic Kenny Kingston was born to the seventh daughter of a seventh daughter — a very psychic sign.

He credits three women in his life with helping him to develop his psychic ability: his grandmother, Catherine Walsh Clark, taught him to read tea leaves when he was four years old; his beloved mother Kaye taught him psychometry (touching an object and picking up psychic vibrations from it) when he was seven; and legendary film immortal (and family friend) Mae West taught him clairaudio (listening to a voice and picking up psychic vibrations) when he was nine years old.

KENNY KINGSTON
Legendary Celebrity Psychic / Medium

Throughout his childhood and as a young adult, Kenny gave psychic messages and readings to friends and neighbors, many of whom were involved in politics and show business. Word spread and soon he was performing on radio and television, as well as appearing live in lectures.

Kenny has appeared on more television shows than any other psychic, guesting repeatedly on major talk shows around the world. He has hosted his own television series twice — *Kenny Kingston: A Psychic Experience* in the late 1970s in the Los Angeles area; and the syndicated *Kenny Kingston Show* on the East coast during the 1990s.

Kenny has given readings and messages to Marilyn Monroe (he was her one and only psychic), Lucille Ball, Greta Garbo, U. S. Presidents Eisenhower and Truman, Whoopi Goldberg, Phyllis Diller, Howie Mandel, Cindy Williams, and many others. His ties to British royalty began with the Duke and Duchess of Windsor and continued to other members of the monarchy. He has written five books on the psychic world, including his best selling book, *I Still Talk To*.

Kenny lives by the motto: "Only Believe, All Things are Possible if You Only Believe."

Victoria Gross

Paranormal researcher and investigator Victoria Gross has been doing professional psychic readings since 1987. Her background is in Tarot, Palmistry, Crystal Gazing, and Psychometry. She also teaches, lectures, and does workshops on these and various subjects relating to metaphysics. Victoria trained at The Arthur Findlay College in England for mediumship, is the founder of The North Orange County Tarot Society located in Southern California, and a member of The International Paranormal Research Organization.

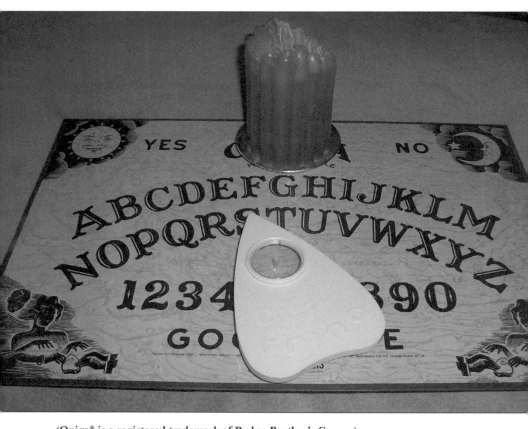

(Ouiga® is a registered trademark of Parker Brother's Games.)

Glossary of Terms

An **Anomaly**, in paranormal terms, refers to any phenomena that we cannot explain.

An **Apparition** refers to any ghost that seems to have material substance. If it appears in any physical form, including a vapor-like image, it may be called an apparition. It can also be explained as the visual appearance of a person whose physical body is not present.

Chinese whisper syndrome refers to a game in which each successive participant secretly whispers to the next a phrase or sentence whispered to them by the preceding participant. Cumulative errors from mishearing often result in the sentence heard by the last player differing greatly and amusingly from the one uttered by the first.

Clearing, or space clearing is the process of ridding an area of lingering unpleasant energy. Space clearing may encourage ghosts to cross over, or at least to leave the haunted location. At times, though, attempting to clear a space of an unwanted spirit may result in even stronger activity than before for an extended period of time.

Demon or Evil Entities seem to be spirits that are either evil in nature, or are actually demons. Demons are commonly considered to be things that have not lived as humans, and seem to take delight in terrorizing humans. Some think demons may even be able to interfere with and effect human kind.

Earthbound Spirits are people who have passed over but do not realize their true condition or choose to stick around and impose themselves on the living. The result is hauntings and occasionally possessions.

Ectoplasm is the physical residue of psychic energy. Ectoplasm can be seen by the naked eye, and is best viewed in dark settings since it is translucent and tends to glow.

EVP (Electronic Voice Phenomena) is the recording of unexplained voices, usually in haunted settings. Many times, no sound is heard while the recording is being made. It's only upon playback that the voices can be heard.

An **Entity** is something that has a distinct, separate existence from our own.

A **Ghost** is a sentient entity or spirit that visits or lingers in our world, after he or she lived among us as a human being. There is also evidence of ghostly animals. It is a form of apparition, usually the visual appearance of a deceased human's spirit or soul.

Haunting describes a setting where ghosts, poltergeists, and/or residual energy seem to produce significant paranormal activity. Recurrent sounds of human activity, sightings of apparitions, and other psychic phenomena, in a location when no one is there physically are all signs of a haunting.

Intelligent Hauntings may be by a ghost or a demon. With an intelligent haunting the entity is aware of its surroundings, including living people who may be present. This entity may be either benevolent, malevolent, or benign.

Malevolent Hauntings are done by a ghost or demon that seeks to inflict harm on the living.

Manifestation is the materialized form of a spirit.

A **Medium** is a person who possesses the ability to communicate with spirits of the deceased. Some mediums claim to be able to channel the spirit, by allowing the deceased to speak or write messages using the medium's body.

Orbs are round, whitish or pastel-colored translucent areas that appear as balls of light and may occasionally seem to be moving. While there has been no substantial proof that the balls of light are associated with ghosts, the dead or any paranormal behavior, many believe that orbs are the human soul or life force of those that once inhabited a physical body here on earth.

The Other Side is a term used to describe the spirit world, or the place spirits go after death beyond our physical plane.

In the word **Paranormal**, the prefix, "para" indicates something that is irregular, faulty, or operating outside the usual boundaries. Paranormal is an umbrella term used to describe a wide variety of reported anomalous phenomena. According to the Journal of Parapsychology, the term paranormal describes "any phenomenon that in one or more respects exceeds the limits of what is deemed physically possible according to current scientific assumptions."

Phenomenon is an unusual, profound, or unexplainable fact or occurrence.

Place memory is information about past events that is stored in the physical environment.

The word **Poltergeist** comes from the German meaning "noisy ghost." This term has been in use since the early nineteenth century to mean a spirit that makes noise, or otherwise plays pranks and is often annoying. Poltergeists can move from one location to another, following the person they've chosen to torment.

A **Portal** literally means a doorway or gate, and in paranormal terms it suggests a specific location through which spirits enter and leave our world. When there are multiple phenomena in a confined area, such as an abundance of unexplained orbs, some people call this a "ghost portal."

Psychic is a word used to describe an occurrence, ability, or event that is sensed without the use of the five known human senses of sight, hearing, taste, touch, and smell. People who are said to possess psychic abilities are referred to as "psychics."

With **Residual Energy**, many believe that emotionally charged events leave an imprint or energy residue on the physical objects nearby.

Residual Haunting is a term used to describe a ghost that is trapped in a continuous loop. Another theory is that an event left a psychic impression on an area and some people are able to witness a replay of that scene. What distinguishes residual energy from an active haunting is that the energy/impressions repeat consistently, as if on a loop. The energy levels may increase or decrease, but the content remains the same with each manifestation. By contrast, in what we term an active haunting, the ghost may respond to environmental stimuli and direct contact.

Spirit is a word that comes from the Latin, meaning "that which animates life", or "the soul of the being." In paranormal terms, spirits are electromagnetic entities in the forms of orbs, mist, vortexes, or shadows, which are the signature of a once-living person who has returned to a specific location. Their nature is interactive as opposed to residual.

Spirit photography captures the image of a ghost on film. Many of these are supposedly intended as a mere portrait of a living human being, but when the film is developed, an ethereal ghostly face or figure can be seen hovering near the subject. This may also incorporate orbs, vortexes, and mists to some degree.

Supernatural is an occurrence in violation of the laws of nature. Spiritualism contends that the phenomena of the séance room are ruled by as yet unknown laws and rejects the term.

"THAT'S ALL FOLKS"
MEL BLANC
MAN OF 1000 VOICES
BELOVED HUSBAND AND FATHER
1908 — 1989

That's All Folks!

Bibliography

Books

Barron's, Cut!, New York: Barron's, 2005

Benoit, Todd. Where Are They Buried? How Did They Die? New York: Black Dog & Leventhal. 2003

Gordon, William A. The Ultimate Hollywood Tour Book. Lake Forest: North Ridge Books, 2006

Guiley, Rosemary Ellen. The Encyclopedia of Ghosts and Spirits. New York: Checkmark Books, 2000.

Hauck, Dennis William. Haunted Places: The National Directory New York: Penguin Books, 1996

Holzer, Hans, Ghosts. New York: Black Dog & Leventhal, 2004.

Jacobson, Laurie, Hollywood Haunted. Los Angeles: Angel City Press, 1994.

Lamparski, Richard, Lamparski's Hidden Hollywood. New York: Simon and Schuster, 1981.

Mead, Robin, Haunted Hotels. Nashville: Rutledge Hill Press, 1995

Parish, James Robert, The Hollywood Book of Death

Schessler, Ken, This is Hollywood. Redlands: Ken Schlesser, 2003

Smith, Barbara, Ghost Stories of Hollywood. New York: McGraw-Hill, 2002.

Wlodarski, Robert and Anne, California Hauntspitality. Alton: Whitechapel Productions Press, 2002.

Wlodarski, Robert and Anne, Haunted Catalina. West Hills: Ghost Publishing, 2000.

Websites

http://campuscircle.net/advertising/hollywoodland/Hollywood_Walking_Tour.pdf

http://catalog1.lapl.org:80/cgi-bin/cw_cgi?fullRecord+11911+968+41225+6+0

http://cinematreasures.org/theater/9863/

http://en.allexperts.com/e/h/ho/hollywood,_los_angeles,_california.htm

http://en.wikipedia.org/wiki/Bessie_Love

http://en.wikipedia.org/wiki/Beverly_Hills,_California
http://en.wikipedia.org/wiki/Bugsy_Siegel
http://en.wikipedia.org/wiki/Elmer_McCurdy
http://en.wikipedia.org/wiki/Frances_Farmer
http://en.wikipedia.org/wiki/George_Harrison
http://en.wikipedia.org/wiki/Gia_Scala
http://en.wikipedia.org/wiki/Hollywood_and_Vine
http://en.wikipedia.org/wiki/Inger_Stevens
http://en.wikipedia.org/wiki/Lupe_V%C3%A9lez
http://en.wikipedia.org/wiki/Natalie_Wood
http://en.wikipedia.org/wiki/Poltergeist_curse
http://en.wikipedia.org/wiki/Ram%C3%B3n_Novarro
http://en.wikipedia.org/wiki/Santa_Catalina_Island,_California
http://en.wikipedia.org/wiki/Thomas_Noguchi
http://en.wikipedia.org/wiki/Tiburcio_Vasquez
http://english.glendale.cc.ca.us/curse.html
http://entertainment.ivillage.com/features/0,,q462,00.html
http://graphic.pepperdine.edu/ane/2005/2005-10-27-haunted.htm*
http://home.hiwaay.net/~oliver/tbintro.htm
http://movies.yahoo.com/movie/1802813191/cast
http://paranormal.about.com/cs/trueghoststories/a/aa022304_2.htm
http://paranormal.about.com/cs/trueghoststories/a/aa022304_2.htm
http://paranormal.about.com/cs/trueghoststories/a/aa022304_3.htm
http://paranormal.about.com/gi/dynamic/offsite.htm?zi=1/XJ&sdn=p
aranormal&cdn=newsissues&tm=82&f=11&su=p284.5.420.ip_&tt=
2&bt=1&bts=1&zu=http%3A//www.women.com/celebs/celebspecial/
articles/0%2C%2C592831_597782%2C00.html
http://pro.imdb.com/name/nm0000015/trivia
http://pro.imdb.com/name/nm0000081/trivia
http://pro.imdb.com/name/nm0000543/trivia
http://pro.imdb.com/name/nm0258201/trivia
http://pro.imdb.com/title/tt0016220/trivia
http://pro.imdb.com/title/tt0049092/trivia
http://pro.imdb.com/title/tt0070047/trivia
http://thehollywoodmuseum.com/welcome.shtml
http://thelongestlistofthelongeststuffatthelongestdomainnameatlonglast.
com/haunted4.html
http://theshadowlands.net/places/california1.htm
http://travel.discovery.com/tv/most-haunted/live-US/cams/cams.html
http://www.allstays.com/Haunted/ca_hollywood_roosevelt.htm
http://www.answers.com/Los%20Angeles%20City%20Fire%20Departm
ent
http://www.answers.com/topic/errol-flynn
http://www.avalonhollywood.com/pdf/Trivia.pdf
http://www.barneysbeanery.com/bb.html

http://www.bbc.co.uk/dna/h2g2/A13645208
http://www.billybobthornton.net/music%20cave.html
http://www.brainyquote.com/quotes/authors/l/lupe_velez.html
http://www.calarchives4u.com/women/whotxt/whotrans.html
http://www.californiahistory.com/sample.html
http://www.carlabaron.net/forum/showthread.php?t=325
http://www.carpenoctem.tv/haunt/ca/
http://www.coastmagazine.com/archive/pre_dec05/travel_santamonica_7.04.html
http://www.crimelibrary.com/notorious_murders/classics/haunted_crime_scene2/4.html
http://www.debased.com/content/celebrities/m/jayne-mansfield.html
http://www.discoverhollywood.com/pagemanager/templates/content.asp?articleid=17&zoneid=1
http://www.dvdtalk.com/dvdsavant/s77bronson.html
http://www.emporis.com/en/wm/bu/?id=116599
http://www.escendi.com.au/eyescream/movies/polt.html
http://www.findadeath.com/Deceased/g/irene/irenegibbons.htm
http://www.findadeath.com/Deceased/m/Vic%20Morrow/vic_morrow.htm
http://www.forteantimes.com/articles/202_magic1.shtml
http://www.frommers.com/destinations/losangeles/D40927.html
http://www.georgianhotel.com/historic.htm
http://www.ghost2ghost.org/calist/calist.htm
http://www.ghostvillage.com/links/links_media.shtml
http://www.herecomestheguide.com/location/detail/wattles-mansion
http://www.highlandgardenshotel.com/
http://www.hollywoodland.org/history.htm
http://www.hollywoodpost43.org/
http://www.imdb.com/name/nm0497372/bio
http://www.ispr.net/news/articles/HouseofFisher.html
http://www.lacitybeat.com/article.php?id=4911&IssueNum=189
http://www.lafeber.com/Lafeber-Library/sevendays.asp
http://www.laokay.com/halac/RanchoLaBrea.htm
http://www.lapetcemetery.com/
http://www.lapressroom.info/Article.aspx?id=10205
http://www.lasplash.com/publish/Los_Angeles_Entertainment_109/Haunted_Hollywood.php
http://www.latimemachines.com/new_page_41.htm
http://www.latimemachines.com/new_page_8.htm
http://www.latirnes.com/news/local/la-me-haunted30oct30/
http://www.latirnes.com/news/local/la-me-haunted30oct30/
http://www.latourist.com/haunted-hollywood.htm
http://www.laurelcanyon.org/20cHist.html
http://www.legendsofamerica.com/CA-Georgianotel.html

http://www.legendsofamerica.com/CA-HauntedHotels3.html
http://www.legendsofamerica.com/GH-CelebrityGhosts3.html
http://www.millikanalumni.com/Pike/Mystery.html
http://www.nndb.com/people/532/000024460/
http://www.npr.org/templates/story/story.php?storyId=6624971
http://www.officialjanis.com/bio.html
http://www.omegaroom.com/ORBsubmit.htm
http://www.paranormalmagazine.com/
http://www.prairieghosts.com/hollywood10.html
http://www.prairieghosts.com/hollywood5.html
http://www.prairieghosts.com/hollywood6.html
http://www.prairieghosts.com/hollywood7.html
http://www.psychics.co.uk/ghosts/mickjagger.html
http://www.samsloan.com/cursed.htm
http://www.seeing-stars.com/Dine2/Musso&Frank.shtml
http://www.sfgate.com/cgi-bin/article.cgi?f=/chronicle/archive/2005/01/30/MNGD5B1PIL1.DTL
http://www.snopes.com/movies/films/polter.htm
http://www.squidoo.com/HauntedNYC/
http://www.starpulse.com/Actors/Novarro,_Ramon/Biography/
http://www.swingdjs.com/phpbb2/viewtopic.php?t=1506&sid=7bd4d3562aa376c780655ca07b58340d
http://www.tributemosthaunted.co.uk/series6.htm
http://www.ulwaf.com/LA-1900s/05.02.html
http://www.unexplainable.net/artman/publish/article_5411.shtml
http://www.unknownmagazine.com/
http://www.victoriam.net/62231.html
http://www.warriorfilmmakers.com/errolflynn/bio/index.html
http://www.yamashirorestaurant.com/
http://you-are-here.com/hollywood/index.html

Index